CAT CRAFTS

CAT CRAFTS

More Than 50 Purrfect Projects

Dawn Cusick

Sterling Publishing Co., Inc. New York
A Sterling/Lark Book

Art Direction: Dana Irwin

Photography: Evan Bracken, Light Reflections

Editorial Assistance: Laura Dover

Production: Dana Irwin, Charlie Covington, Bobby Gold

Illustrations: Charlie Covington, Bobby Gold

Proofreading: Julie Brown

Library of Congress Cataloging-in-Publication Data

Cusick, Dawn.

    Cat crafts : more than 50 purrfect projects / Dawn Cusick.
        p. cm.
    "A Sterling/Lark book."
    Includes index.
    ISBN 0-8069-9533-X
    1. Cats—Equipment and supplies. 2. Handicraft. 3. Gifts.
    I. Title.
    SF447.3.C87 1997
    745.5—dc20   96-35792
                                             CIP

10 9 8 7 6 5 4 3 2

A Sterling/Lark Book

Published by Sterling Publishing Co., Inc.

387 Park Avenue South, New York, NY 10016

Created and produced by Altamont Press, Inc.

50 College Street, Asheville, NC 28801

© 1997, Altamont Press

Distributed in Canada by Sterling Publishing,

      c/o Canadian Manda Group, One Atlantic Ave., Suite 105, Toronto, Canada M6K 3E7

Distributed in Great Britain and Europe by Cassell PLC

   Wellington House, 125 Strand, London WC2R 0BB, England

Distributed in Australia by Capricorn Link (Australia) Pty Ltd., P.O. Box 6651, Baulkam Hills, Business Centre, NSW 2153, Australia

Every effort has been made to ensure that all the information in this book is accurate. However, due to differing conditions, tools, and individual skills, the publisher cannot be responsible for any injuries, losses, or other damages that may result from the use of the information in this book.

Contents

Cats have been the highlight of my life for as long as I can remember. As a child, I snuck more than my fair share of kittens into the house. By far the best cat was Sir Puss 'n Boots – Kitty Boots for short – who set an all-time family record one night by giving me eighty-seven forehead kisses from the front door to the kitchen. A later addition to the family, Miss Lady Slippers, inspired my mother's impromptu birds-and-the-bees discussion. "See," she pointed out when Lady's first heat brought lots of gentlemen callers, "they love her now, but how many of them will stick around when she's pregnant?" Sure enough, eight weeks later, Lady's sides were bulging and nary a gentleman caller could be seen. I got the point.

Years later and true to familial form, my parents' only concern about my choice of a life partner was not his education, his career goals, or his life ambitions. "He's not a cat person," is how my father summed it up. (Perhaps the large black dog who always rode in his passenger seat gave him away.) In retrospect, my parents were right. Living with a dog person has its challenges. Fortunately, we've never had a formal discussion about how the children should be raised, and my sweetheart has been remarkably blind to the cat propaganda I've heaped upon the children. They are definitely cat people now.

Hearing similar cat tales from the designers who contributed projects to this book has been great fun. Some of the projects, such as the tile cat house, the Christmas stockings, and the pompom tease puffs were created as labors of love for the designers' personal cats. Other projects, such as the cat jewelry, wall hangings, and pillows, were designed as glorious celebrations of the feline species. Feel free to adapt the projects as you like or use them as creative springboards for your own ideas.

A special thanks to Carol Taylor, whose innocent lunchtime question – "Wouldn't it be fun to do crafts for cats?" – led to this book.

Many thanks to the following contributing designers . . .

HEATHER ALLEN is a studio artist specializing in rag rugs, surface design, and papermaking. Her first book, a collection of contemporary rag rugs and how-to techniques, will be published by Lark Books in fall 1997.

NANCY ASMUS has won numerous awards for her sewing skills at the local and state level. She resides in Conneaut Lake, Pennsylvania, and is currently designing a line of patterns that she plans to publish next year.

BRENNA BUSSE has made hundreds of handmade dolls, many of them using recycled materials such as springs, zippers, and buttons. Her button dolls appear in The Button Craft Book, Sterling Publishing Co., Inc., 1995.

EVANS R. CARTER is a college student who loves making things with her hands. Codesigner Gus Adams is a furniture refinisher who enjoys tackling new projects. The tile house will be home to two new kittens.

CENTRAL HAYWOOD HIGH's Spanish students and their teacher, Laura Rogers, worked together on cat and mouse pinatas. Adam Hawkins, Chucky Norris, Matt Oliver, Lisa Ford, Richie Moon, and Michael Rogers contributed to the project.

CHRIS NOAH-COOPER specializes in cut and pierced-paper lamp shades, scherenschnitte, etchings, and faux finished frames. An art teacher and art therapist, her work has appeared in *Better Homes and Gardens* magazine. She resides in Miamisburg, Ohio, with her two cats, Mario and Fang.

SUSAN DRISCOLL resides in Asheville, North Carolina. She is owned by two cats, Amanda and Mona.

ALICE ENSLEY enjoys dabbling in a wide variety of crafts, from sewing to nature crafts, as well as experimenting with new materials and techniques. She lives in Clyde, North Carolina.

GAY FAY is an Austin, Texas, artist whose indulgences transferred several years ago from felines to children, much to her cats' dismay. The kitty contingent was further traumatized by the addition of lizards, guinea pigs, and a dog. Now that her children are old enough to enjoy pussycat pampering, equanimity has been restored.

NORRIS HALL creates wood jewelry, furniture, and sculpture from his studio in Murfreesboro, Tennessee.

MIKE HESTER owns and operates Hester's Lothlorien, a custom woodworking business featuring native hardwoods, in Asheville, North Carolina. Mike insists that his new cat, Cassey, actually sways like a professional boxer when she walks.

SUSAN KINNEY is a papermaker, a potter, a jeweler, and an interior designer living in Asheville, North Carolina. Her six indoor Persians and two outdoor cats served as inspiration for her projects.

BETTY KERSHNER creates custom hand painted clothing and accessories as well as commissioned wall hangings and banners. She lives in Sewanee, Tennessee, where she frequently gives workshops in handpainting on fabric.

CLAUDIA LEE, a handmade paper artist from Kingsport, Tennessee, admits to loving the textures, colors, and immediacy of papermaking materials. She offers workshops and demonstrations across the country, and her work is featured in *Fiberarts Design Book IV.*

MARY MARTIN designs and hand paints her line of cat jewelry from her home in Columbus, Georgia. All of her pieces are originals, and each is named after a cat she's known.

LAUREY MASTERTON creates luscious treats for people and cats through her business, Laurey's Catering, in Asheville, North Carolina. Her projects were developed and styled with Monroe Moore, a cat lover and food stylist living in Asheville, North Carolina.

KIT MECKLEY has always enjoyed collecting interesting natural materials, and her craft projects are usually inspired by her collections.

GENNA MILES, of Manteo, North Carolina, spins dog and cat hair to create custom hats for a variety of customers. She also teaches spinning in the public schools and offers workshops. She laments that her two cats, Fluffy and Flakey, are too shorthaired to contribute fur for spinning.

DOLLY LUTZ MORRIS creates dried flower designs and handcrafted dolls from her home in rural Saegertown, Pennsylvania. She is the author of the *Flower Drying Handbook*, Sterling Publishing Co., Inc, 1996. She is the proud owner of eight cats.

ALYCE NADEAU grows more than 200 different herbs for her business, Goldenrod Mountain Herbs, in Lansing, North Carolina, where she makes and markets herbal crafts. She is the author of *Making and Selling Herbal Crafts*, Sterling Publishing Co., Inc., 1996.

LEAH NALL owns and operates a custom upholstering and a custom lamp shade company from her studio in Fairhope, Alabama. Her eight-year-old Abyssinian, Tangens Locus Wildtype, a passionate lizard huntress, served as inspiration for her projects.

BOBBE NEEDHAM participates in the Foster Pet Program in Asheville, North Carolina. She is currently writing *Dog Crafts: More Than 50 Grrreat Projects*, to be published by Sterling Publishing Co. in the spring of 1997.

CAROLINE OTTINGER has a background in graphic design and illustration. She resides in Waynesville, North Carolina, and enjoys all crafts. Her favorite feline, Cygnnet, is particularly fond of her cat crafts.

MARY PARKER pursues a career in public sector finance in order to indulge her passion for fabric. She lives in Asheville, North Carolina, with five well-fed cats and the "world's best husband."

CATHERINE REURS is an internationally recognized needlepoint and cross-stitch designer. Her second book, *Splendid Needlepoint*, will be published by Lark Books in spring 1997. Her designs are available as needlepoint kits and cross-stitch charts. For a color catalog, write: Catherine Reurs Needlepoint/In Splendid Detail, Ltd, 50 Marion Road, Watertown, MA 02172-4737.

MARY SAVAGE, a clothing/craft designer and stylist from Spring Green, Wisconsin, is the proud parent of four new kittens. She and her family recently said farewell to Sherri, a shorthaired tabby who had been a part of her family for many years.

KIM SHUCK is a basketmaker, a bead artist, and a Native American craft educator from San Francisco, California. She is a frequent contributor to craft books.

JUDITH STOLL is a passionate gardener, cat lover, and freelance writer living in Saegertown, Pennsylvania.

TERRY TAYLOR works for the Lark Books catalog in Asheville, North Carolina, as the craft coordinator. His mosaic cat memorial was made to honor Kitty, a large, one-eyed marmalade cat who is dearly missed.

CARL THOMAS, who began his woodworking career years ago as a ship's carpenter, is a custom woodworker residing in Fairhope, Alabama. He enjoys large projects, such as building staircases, as well as smaller projects, such as building couches for cats.

SUZANN THOMPSON, whose fish blanket was designed for Monsanto's Designs for America Program, has always liked cats. Nevertheless, her three pets are d—gs. Suzann and her husband, daughter, and um, animals are Texas natives but live in Sheffield, England.

KIM TIBBALS-THOMPSON is a graphic artist and art director who also enjoys drawing, sewing, herbal crafts, gardening, and broom making. She resides in Waynesville, North Carolina.

VAN THOMPSON is the proud owner of Crazy Bread, an orange tabby named after a television commercial. He resides in Garland, Texas.

MARYN WYNNE owns and operates Flytes of Fancy, a feline and canine clothing accessory business, with her mother, Liz Fye, in Lakeville, Minnesota.

M o d e l s . . .

Many thanks to the following talented cats and their patient stage parents for lending their modeling talents . . .

BUSTER BELL, a red male Persian, presides over three other cats in his home in Asheville, North Carolina. Christa Bell, one of Buster's roommates, is a Chocolate Point Siamese.

BAMBI BONNER recently had the good sense to change families when her former owner married someone who is not a cat person. She likes car rides, batting toys around the house, and leaping into the air to catch balls.

PANTHER CASON, a five-year-old black shorthair, is the ever-so-pampered baby of high-school senior Jennifer Cason, who received him as a gift on her 12th birthday. Despite his ferocious name, Panther's usual prey consists of butterflies and two family dogs.

MISS KITTY FRANKLIN resides with her family of three dogs, a bird, and two humans in Marion, North Carolina. She was rescued as an orphaned kitten two years ago and suffers from a complete hearing loss.

MAYA, ZACH, AND CHELSEA ROSE KINNEY are now adult cats living in North Carolina, California, and Georgia.

ELEKTRA LUND is a former Nebraska farm cat who was bottle-fed as a kitten and still enjoys being held like a baby. Her favorite activities include playing with the answering machine and making her family laugh.

EMMA, HOBY, MOO, STUART, AND BLACK KITTY are the curious and energetic kittens of mama cat Sherman Woodsen, who was rescued as an abandoned cat in Sherman, Texas.

Ophelia and Josephine McDaniel were nurtured by people after the premature death of their mother. Lucy is a visiting houseguest who summers with her grandparents.

Also thanks to snapshot models Sarton, Max, Tipper, and Fergie.

So many cats, so little space . . . Special thanks to the felines of the world who are not represented in these pages, including: Kitty Boots, Lady Slippers, Tigger Ray Mouse, Ike, Sweetheart, Kashmir, Pharlap, Minnie, Sam, Tuesday, Gorby, Oscar, Midnight, Mugsie, Cassio, Nagi, George, Ophelia, Josephine, Spooky, Big Kitty, Little Kitty, Alley, Razzle, Pooh, Barney, Blanca, Sallie, Pratt, Whitneys, Spirit, Booster, Boobareen, Simon, Callie, Cadburry, Jonathon, Princess, Golda Alexander, Marble, Bubba, Janeway, Picard, Kitty, Scooter, Sir Brasstopher Lyone, Oliver, Dromios, Cleo, King Casey, Jasper, Sneaker, Winston, Emma Lee, Garfield, Priscilla, Tarantella, Reuben King, Comet, Cupid, Tubby, Boots, Hobbes, Playful, Abigale, Emily and Baby Kitty.

Tepee Playhouse

MATERIALS

3 heavy, rough-textured place mats or 3 pieces of sisal or other rug remnant

Heavy cardboard (the largest sheet you can find)

2 old towels in a color that contrasts well with the place mats

3 yards (2.7 m) 5/8" (15 mm) cotton ribbon

Multi-purpose craft glue

Feathers

1

Place all three mats or carpet remnants on the cardboard and trace them, adding at least 6" (15 cm) to the ends for bottom overlap. Score lightly between the middle mat.

2

Cut the toweling to fit the cardboard and glue it to the front and back sides. Trim the edges with the ribbon, then glue the mats in the center of each section.

3

Fold the cardboard into a triangular, tepee shape and glue the extra flaps to the bottom. Sew several feathers to one end of a 16" (41 cm) length of ribbon, then stitch the ribbon to the top of the tepee and reinforce with hot glue.

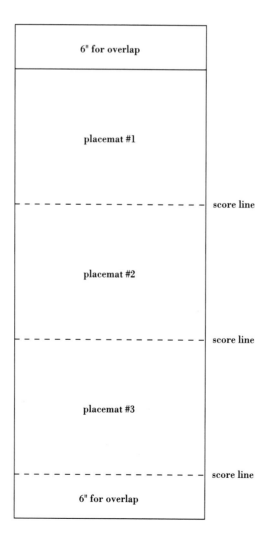

6" for overlap

placemat #1

score line

placemat #2

score line

placemat #3

score line

6" for overlap

DESIGN
SUSAN KINNEY

Cat Nap Box

MATERIALS

Sturdy cardboard box
Roll of kraft paper
Clear-drying craft glue
3/4 yard (.7 m) colorful fabric with a tight weave
Pillow stuffing
1/8" (3 mm) satin ribbon (enough to go around the box three times)
Clear acrylic spray

1

Cut the sides of the box down to about 5" (13 cm) high. (You may wish to make the sides an inch or two higher if you have an especially robust kitty.) Tear the kraft paper into enough small pieces ranging in size from 3 x 3" to 3 x 6" (7.5 x 7.5 to 7.5 x 15 cm).

2

Pour some of the glue into a bowl and thin it with water until it's an easily brushable consistency. Place one of the longer strips on a smooth, washable surface and brush glue onto the back. Center the strip over the top of the open edge and smooth down on both sides of the box. Continue working in this manner, overlapping the paper pieces as you work, until you've covered all of the inside surface area. Press out any air bubbles and smooth down any loose pieces. Allow the box to dry

completely, then repeat the process to cover the outer and bottom surface areas.

3

Prewash and iron the fabric. Measure and cut a 3" border strip long enough to fit each of the long and short sides of the box, adding an extra inch to each of the long strips. Measure and mark a line around the box 1-1/2" (4 cm) down from the top edge.

4

Brush the water-diluted glue onto the marked border area of one of the long edges. Press the fabric into the glue, taking care to align the bottom edge with your measured markings and allowing a 1/2" (12 mm) overlap on each end. Smooth the fabric with a downward motion. Brush glue onto the inside of the box. Fold the fabric over the edge and smooth in place with a downward motion. Repeat on the second long side, then repeat on the short sides.

5

Play with placement of the cat motif on page 115 to determine how many you will need. Photocopy the motifs onto a contrasting color of paper, enlarging or reducing the size if desired and cut them out. Measure and draw a guideline 1/4" (6 mm) up from the bottom

of the box all the way around. Brush glue onto the back of each cat and press them in place one at a time, taking care to line their paws up with the guide line and pat them down with a damp sponge. Allow the glue to completely dry.

6

Glue a length of satin ribbon over the guideline all the way around the box, starting at the corner of one of the long sides and working your way around until you reach the starting point. Allow the ends to overlap about 1" and glue them down. Repeat this process to finish the raw fabric edges on both the inside and outside edges. Allow the glue to completely dry.

7

Coat the entire box with a thin layer of glue, working on one side at a time and allowing it to dry before moving on to the next side. Allow the glue to completely dry, then finish with two or three light coats of clear

acrylic sealer, allowing the sealer to completely dry between coats.

8

To make the cushion, measure the inside of the box and add 1-1/2" to all sides. Cut two pieces of fabric to these measurements. Sew the two pieces together with right sides facing with a 1/4" seam allowance, leaving a 4" opening for turning. Clip the corner points, turn right side out, and press. Stuff the cushion and slip stitch the opening closed.

9

Sit down with your cat for a serious discussion. Explain that this box is very special and is off limits for cats. Leave the room and wait for your cat to claim the box.

DESIGN
LIZ FYE

"ARE YOU SITTING IN THE
CATBIRD-SEAT?" — JAMES
THURBER, "THE CATBIRD SEAT"

Cat and Mouse Piñatas

MATERIALS

Package of balloons in assorted sizes

Masking tape

White craft glue or wallpaper paste

Newspaper

Gesso

Acrylic or poster paints

Sheet of construction paper in a bright color

Four or five colors of tissue paper

1

For the cat piñata, blow up two circular balloons, one for the body and a smaller one for the head. Tape the two balloons together. For the mouse, blow up a small circular balloon for the head and a long, tubular-shaped balloon for the body. Tape the two balloons together.

2

Prepare a mache mixture by diluting white craft glue or wallpaper paste with water to a loose consistency. Tear the newspaper into 1 - 2" (2.5 - 5 cm) strips. Dip a strip of newspaper in the mixture and squeeze out any excess liquid by running it through your fingers.

3

Place the strip over the balloon mold. Repeat the process with additional newspaper strips until you've covered the mold four or five times, alternating the direction of the strips with each layer. Allow the mache to completely dry.

4

Cut a 1 x 2" opening in an inconspicuous place, leaving one side uncut. Coat the entire mache piece with a generous layer of gesso to prevent the newsprint from showing through the finished pieces. Allow the gesso to completely dry.

5

Paint the cat and mouse as desired. Cut ears and facial features if desired from the construction paper and glue in place. Stack the tissue paper sheets on top of each other and cut out a strip long enough to fit around the neck area and 3 to 4" (7.5 - 10 cm) wide. Fold the strip in half lengthwise and make evenly spaced cuts in the tissue, leaving about 1/2" (12 mm) of the folded area uncut. Glue around the neck.

6

Form tails with multicolored strips of tissue paper and glue them in place. For a finishing touch on the mouse, cut circles with a 5" (13 cm) diameter from several colors of paper. Gather the circle at the center and glue in place.

7

Fill the piñata with kitty and/or people treats and enjoy the party.

DESIGN
CENTRAL HAYWOOD HIGH
SPANISH STUDENTS

Catnip Mice

MATERIALS

Cotton fabric scraps

4 - 5" (10 - 13 cm) lengths of leather or yarn scraps

Dried catnip leaves and blooms

1

Cut out the mouse shape from doubled fabric and pin the pieces together with right sides facing, positioning the tail as desired. (See pattern on page 125.) Stitch together with a narrow seam allowance, leaving an opening large enough for turning.

2

Trim seams and turn right side out. Stuff the mouse with dried catnip and slip-stitch the opening closed.

> "CATS DO NOT KEEP THE MICE AWAY; . . . THEY PRESERVE THEM FOR THE CHASE."
> — OSWALD BARRON

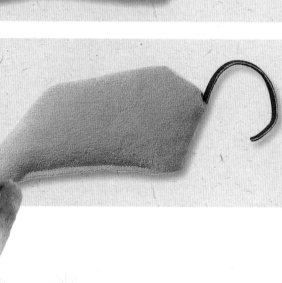

DESIGN
ALYCE NADEAU

MATERIALS FOR SIX ORNAMENTS

6 slices of bread
3 egg whites
Birdseed or thistle seed
Fine-gauge floral wire
Assorted ribbons

1

Trace the cat shapes on page 125 onto a piece of paper, then cut them out and trace them onto the bread slices. Carefully cut out the bread with a sharp knife.

2

Fold the birdseed into the egg whites and press it gently into the bread. Bake the ornaments at 350° (180 C) for ten minutes. Allow them to completely cool.

3

Cut a 6" (15 cm) length of floral wire for each ornament. Gently insert one end of the wire through the top of each ornament at least 1/4" (6 mm) in from the edge. Form the wire into a loop and twist the ends together to secure. If desired, hot-glue a colorful ribbon to the base of the wire or around the cat's neck. Hang the ornaments outside a window that your cat likes to frequent.

> **"IF CATS HAD WINGS THERE WOULD BE NO DUCKS IN THE LAKE."**
> — INDIAN PROVERB

DESIGN
ALICE ENSLEY,
APRIL ENSLEY

17

Litter Box Privacy Screen

MATERIALS

5' (1.5 m) piece 1 x 12" (2.5 x 30 cm) yellow pine (planed to 1/2" (12 mm) thickness) or a 5' piece of 11-1/4 x 1/2" (28.5 cm x 12 mm) plywood

1/4" (6 mm) template material (posterboard, scrap wood, etc.)

2 pairs of butt hinges

TOOLS

Jigsaw

Router and 1/4" straight bit with guide and 1/4" roundover bit

Drill and 7/8" (21 mm) bit

Chisel, 3/4 to 1" (2 - 2.5 m)

Compass

1

Cut a 20" (51 cm) piece from the board. Mark a 5-5/8" (14 cm) radius from the top. You can cut the radius now or leave it whole until after cutting out the cattail to make clamping and holding easier.

2

Draw and cut a slight curve from the template material 16 - 18" (41 - 46 cm) long to use as a guide for the cattail stems. Cut three slots in the wood using a 1/4" router bit using the template to guide you 14 - 16" (36 x 41 cm) long. (Practice on scrap materials first until you're happy with the effect.)

3

At the top of the grooves, drill two 7/8" holes 3" apart. Draw two straight lines connecting the holes. Jigsaw along the line to complete the cattail.

4

Complete the cattail detailing by making two angled cuts at the top of the cattail with the chisel, leaving a small tip.

5

Cut the center free from the board (if not done earlier) and cut the radius top.

6

Cut two pieces to 14-1/2" (37 cm) and cut the width down to 10" (25 cm). Mark a 10" radius on each board, starting at the top of one edge and working to below the center of the other side. Cut out with a jigsaw.

7

Rout the top and outside edges of the side pieces with a 1/4" roundover bit. Lay the side pieces next to the center piece and mark the area where the side pieces meet. Rout the outside edge above the marks.

8

Rout the tops of the cattails to enhance the design if desired. Sand all pieces, then mount the hinges on the back sides.

DESIGN
MIKE HESTER

19

Kitty Memorial

MATERIALS

6 to 10 ceramic plates, half with motifs and half in solid colors*

1 ceramic kitten* (not a salt or pepper shaker)

8" (20 cm) square concrete paving stone or patio block

Ceramic floor-tile mortar

Sanded ceramic-tile floor grout

Tile nippers

Safety glasses

Spatula

Grout spreader

Water sealant, optional

*Flea markets and garage sales are good sources.

1

Break the solid colored plates into working pieces about 1" (2.5 cm) in size with tile nippers. (Precise sizes are not important; the pieces can be trimmed down later if necessary.) For plates with central motifs, chip away the outer rim of the plate with tile nippers and trim out the motifs.

2

Sort the pieces into two piles, one flat and one non-flat. Rearrange your materials until you're happy with their placement, working first with the kitten, then the motif pieces, and finally the solid colors. Break additional plates if you do not have enough pieces.

3

Mix the mortar according to manufacturer's instructions, adding the dry materials into the liquid until the consistency is that of stiff mashed potatoes. Allow to set up as directed.

4

Apply a small amount of mortar to both the bottom of the kitten and the stone. Press well to ensure a tight bond and remove any excess that squeezes out by spreading it outward from the kitten.

5

Apply a 1/8" (3 mm) thickness of mortar to the remaining top surface of the stone and press in the pieces, allowing 1/4" or less between the tiles. Remove any mortar that squeezes up between the tiles with the edge of a spatula (or with a nail, toothpick, etc.). Allow to dry for at least 24 hours. Repeat the process on the sides if desired.

6

Scratch off any traces of mortar on the tiles and chip away any remaining chunks of mortar. Mix the sanded floor-tile grout according to the manufacturer's instructions, adding the dry materials into the liquid. Allow to set up as directed.

7

Apply floor grout to the spaces between the tiles with a grout spreader. Remove any excess grout from the surface. Remove the grout haze from the tiles as directed. (This usually involves cleaning the tiles with a sponge and water and then polishing with a soft cloth.) Allow to completely dry, then finish with a commercial water sealant if the memorial will be exposed to harsh weather conditions.

DESIGN
TERRY TAYLOR

A Sacred History

Cats have been enjoyed as pets since 2100 B.C. In 450 B.C., the Greek historian Herodotus documented the laws that protected cats. Anyone who killed a cat could be punished by death. When a cat died, the family would often bring the body to Bubastis, the center of worship for the cat goddess Bastet. Here the dead pet was embalmed, wrapped, and laid in a special cat-shaped coffin before being buried in a cat cemetery. In the 19th century, some 300,000 Egyptian cat mummies were shipped to Liverpool, England, where they were turned into fertilizer and sold by the ton.

"I CANNOT EXIST WITHOUT A CAT . . . LIFE WOULD NOT BE WORTH LIVING WITHOUT A CAT."
— PEGGY BACON

Kitty Bowl

MATERIALS

Cat serving bowl

Puff paints in several compatible colors

Small paintbrush

Clear aerosol sealant

1

Photocopy the cat and mouse motifs on page 123 and lightly transfer them onto the bowl with a pencil. Paint a narrow border around the bottom of the bowl in a solid color.

2

Fill in the cat and mouse shapes with a solid color, then add detailing with contrasting colors. Note: You can work puff paints on top of each other when they're still wet if you're careful not to drag the nozzle tip through the base color.

3

Add detailing around the bottom border and near the mice. Spray on a protective layer of clear sealant when the paint has completely dried.

DESIGN
KIM TIBBALS-THOMPSON

Cosmic Kitty Collar and Leash

MATERIALS

Purchased collar and leash in solid colors

Small wood cutouts with predrilled holes, 1 moon and 6 stars in assorted sizes (available in craft shops)

Gold and silver glitter puff paint

Paintbrush

3 jump rings, 2 large and 1 small

1

Paint the moon gold and the stars silver. Add small dots of puff paint to both sides of the moon and one small star, allowing each side to completely dry before painting the other. Add small gold dots to one side of the remaining stars.

2

Hot-glue two large and one small star at the base of the leash handle and hot-glue two stars at the collar end. Thread a large jump ring through the remaining star and moon. Thread these rings onto the smaller jump ring and thread it onto the collar loop.

3

Decorate the collar and leash with dots of silver and gold puff paint, concentrating them closer together near the stars and gradually tapering them off. Add small curls and loops if desired.

DESIGN
KIM TIBBALS-THOMPSON

Tile Cat House

MATERIALS

Sand paper

Small wood dog house

Approximately 40 4" (10 cm) ceramic tiles in bright colors (premium grades are not necessary)

Ceramic floor tile mortar

Sanded ceramic tile floor grout

Tile nippers

Safety glasses

Spatula

Grout spreader

Water sealant

1

Sand the sides, front, and back of the house to create a better adhesion surface for the tiles. Break the tiles into working pieces about 1" (2.5 cm) sin size with tile nippers. (Precise sizes are not important; the pieces can be trimmed down later if necessary.) Sort the tile pieces by color.

2

Enlarge the motifs on page 112 (or use an outline from a book or advertisement) and transfer them onto sides of the house with pencil. Prop the house so you have a flat surface to work on and begin playing with color arrangements until you find a pleasing look.

3

Mix the mortar according to the manufacturer's instructions, adding the dry materials into the liquid until the consistency is that of stiff mashed potatoes. Allow the mortar to set up as directed.

4

Apply a 1/8" (3 mm) thickness of mortar to a small area of the wood surface and press in the tile pieces, allowing 1/4" (6 mm) or less between the tiles. Remove any mortar that squeezes up between the tiles with the edge of a spatula. Cover the remaining surface area and allow the mortar to dry for at least 24 hours. Repeat the process on the front, back, and remaining side.

5

Scratch off any traces of mortar on the tiles and chip away any remaining chunks of mortar. Mix the sanded floor tile grout according to the manufacturer's instructions, adding the dry materials into the liquid. Allow to set up as directed.

6

Mix the floor grout as directed by the manufacturer and spread it over the tiles to fill the spaces. Remove as much of the excess grout as possible with a grout spreader.

7

Remove the haze from the tiles as directed by the manufacture. (This usually in involves cleaning the tiles with a sponge and water and then polishing with a soft cloth.) Allow to completely dry, then finish with a commercial water sealant.

8

Give kitty a tour of the completed tile house. Explain that you realize it's not quite worthy of him/her, but that it is finer than any dog house in the neighborhood.

DESIGN
EVANS R. CARTER AND GUS ADAMS

Tease Puffs

Small bag of pom-poms in assorted sizes

Bamboo or thin wooden dowel at least 24" (60 cm) long

2 yards (1.8 m) durable elastic cording

Tapestry needle

1

Cut three to five lengths of cording ranging from 12 to 40" (30 - 100 cm) in length. Thread the needle with the cording, pierce it through a pom-pom, and knot the end. Repeat with the remaining lengths of cording.

2

Attach the cording to the bamboo by wrapping it around the pole several times, tying off, and reinforcing with hot glue.

DESIGN
SUSAN KINNEY

26

Kitty Pla at

MATERIALS

- *18 x 12" (45 x 30 cm) rectangle of heavy fabric*
- *Fabric paints in desired colors*
- *Small paint brush*
- *Laminating vinyl slightly larger than fabric, optional*
- *Rotary cutter or sharp scissors*

Photocopy   int the background first,
the motifs o   fill in the motifs. Allow
the right sid   aint to completely dry.
ric, taking ca
the design.

2

3

Apply the laminate to the painted fabric, experimenting with a small scrap of painted fabric first. Trim off 1/2" (12 mm) on all edges with a rotary cutter or sharp scissors.

DESIGN
LEAH NALL

Car Cover

Graph paper

*60" (150 cm) wide flag
 bunting or other sturdy
 fabric, approximately 10
 yards (9 m)*

Chalk

*Acrylic fabric paint and
 brush*

1

Measure the following areas
on your vehicle: width and
length of hood area; width
and height of front and
back windshields (Note:
windshields are often a different width at the top than
at the bottom, so measure
both); width and length of
roof, width and length of
side window areas. Estimate
the degree that the front and
back windshields slant.

2

Draw a scaled layout from
your measurements, then
calculate the amount of fabric needed. (See example on
page 114.) Draw a full-sized
pattern on newsprint or pattern paper, adding seam
allowances, hem allowances,
and ease. Cut out your fabric from this pattern.

3

Baste the side panel in place
along the front windshield
and roof area, leaving the
rear windshield seam

28

unsewn. Place the basted cover on your vehicle to determine placement of rear view mirror slits. Slash the fabric from the bottom of the side panel up far enough to allow the rear view mirrors to protrude.

4

To correct any fitting problems, remove your basting threads and mark new stitching lines with pins. Remove the cover and mark the new stitching lines with chalk. Cut a 2" (5 cm) wide fabric strip and bind the slashed areas as you would a sleeve placket. Sew the seams with a regular stitch length, stitching over the basting threads and/or over the chalk marks.

5

Press a hem all around the outside of the cover. Fold under again and machine hem. Make ties from 2" fabric strips to secure the cover to the front bumper, below the rear view mirrors, and along the back windshield. Sew the ties to the hem.

6

Cut a paw-print stencil from the motif on page 110. Position the prints so they appear to be walking up your car, and paint.

The Power of Paw Prints

For some, a hood embellished with paw prints is a symbol of the good life, a sign that the cats in their life truly care. For others, a scattering of paw prints on a freshly washed car is enough to make fur fly . . . literally. And while you may not have found any mountain lion prints on your car lately, even a diehard cat lover can find herself irritated by the claw scratches left in the paint by skidding felines.

The car cover shown left solves all the problems. Your kitty still gets an engine-warmed perch and your car enjoys a protective layer that prevents scratch marks (as well as acid fog and bird droppings) from damaging the surface. If, after enjoying the function and beauty of your own car cover, you find yourself tempted to make one for the crusty, always-complaining-about-your-cat's-footprints-on-his-car-hood dog lover next door, forget it. Some problems are better left unsolved.

Photo Courtesy of American Isuzu Motors, Inc. Graham Westmoreland, photographer.

Romantic Dining
(for People and Cats)

HERRING PATÉ

INGREDIENTS

2 cans white tuna, packed in water

1 stick butter

1 jar herring tidbits, packed in wine

1 jar black lumpfish caviar

1 jar red lumpfish caviar

Parsley, for garnish

1

Melt the butter, then drain the tuna and herring. Blend the tuna, the herring, the butter, and one teaspoon (3 g.) of the black caviar to a thick purée in a food processor.

2

Line a small bread pan with plastic wrap and add the puree. Refrigerate for at least three hours. Turn onto a serving tray.

3

Drain and rinse both colors of caviar in a tea strainer, shaking out all water. Garnish as desired.

SALMON MOUSSE

INGREDIENTS

1 envelope unflavored gelatin

1/4 cup (62 ml.) boiling water

1/4 cup cold water

2 tablespoons (30 ml.) lemon juice

Zest of one lemon

4 oz. (115 g.) of smoked salmon

1/2 cup (125 ml.) mayonnaise

1 tablespoon (10 g.) fresh or dried dill

1 cup (250 ml.) heavy cream

Paprika to taste

1

Dissolve the gelatin in a large bowl with boiling water. Add the cold water, and refrigerate until thick but not completely set, about 20 minutes. (Note: if you get involved in something else and the mixture completely sets, dissolve it over a double boiler and begin again.)

2

Stir in the mayonnaise, the dill, the lemon juice and zest, and the paprika. (Note: If you're making the mousse exclusively for cats, eliminate the lemons, the dill, and the paprika.)

3

Whip the cream to soft peaks and rough-chop the salmon. Fold the cream and the salmon into the gelatin mixture, then place in a fish mold and allow to set for at least 2 hours.

"NOT THAT A CAT'S LIFE IS SO UNBEARABLE,
BUT . . . IT IS FILLED WITH
SO MANY TEMPTATIONS."
— CLAIRE NECKER

31

PARMESAN PUFF PASTRY

INGREDIENTS

Frozen puff pastry sheets
Fish-shaped cookie cutter
Parchment baking paper
Egg
Pastry brush
*Coarsely grated or shred-
 ded Parmesan cheese*

1

Defrost the puff pastry
sheets according to the manufacturer's instructions. Cut
the pastry out with a cookie
cutter.

2

Add 2 tablespoons of water
to the egg and beat with a
fork to make an egg wash.
Paint the wash over the fish
shapes with a pastry brush.

3

Sprinkle Parmesan cheese
over the wash and bake at
375° (190° C) until puffed
and golden.

PARTY PESTO

INGREDIENTS

1/2 pound (230 g.) fresh
  basil leaves (for people)
  OR 1/2 pound fresh cat-
  nip leaves (for cats)

3 cloves garlic

1 stick butter

1/2 cup (125 ml.) extra
  virgin olive oil

1 cup (240 g.) parmesan
  cheese

1/2 cup (76 g.) walnuts or
  pine nuts

1

Blend the ingredients in a
food processor until the
mixture is smooth and
creamy.

2

Serve over a bed of pasta
(for humans) or over a bed
of dried cat food (for cats).

ANCHOVY STRAWS

INGREDIENTS

Frozen puff pastry sheets

Anchovy fillets in strips

Egg

Pastry brush

Pizza cutter or sharp knife

Dried parsley (for human garnish)

Dried catnip (for cat garnish)

Parchment paper

1

Defrost the puff pastry according to the manufacturer's instructions. Cut the sheets in half to form rectangles.

2

Add 2 tablespoons (30 ml.) of water to the egg and beat with a fork to make an egg wash. Paint the wash over the rectangles with a pastry brush.

3

Place the anchovy strips on one half of each rectangle and fold the pastry in half as if you were closing a book.

4

Roll the book shapes out so they stick together, then cut the pastry in thin strips with a pizza cutter. Add a twist to each stick and brush again with the egg wash.

5

Garnish with parsley (for people) or catnip (for cats) and bake on a parchment-paper-lined pan in a 375° (190° C) oven until puffed and golden.

34

ANTIPASTO SALAD

INGREDIENTS

Smoked mussels

Smoked trout fillets

Lobster and salmon paté

Decorative lettuce (for people) OR fresh catnip leaves (for cats)

Lemon slices OR dry cat food

1

Line a serving plate with lettuce or catnip. Arrange mussels, trout, and patés around the greenery.

2

Garnish the platter with lemon slices (for people) or dry cat food (for cats).

DESIGN
LAUREY MASTERTON AND
MONROE MOORE

MATERIALS

FOR COUCH FORM

Cardboard (broken down boxes are fine)

1/3 sheet 1/2" (12 mm) plywood

Sheet of posterboard

1" (2.5 cm) finishing nails

Air nailer and wood glue (optional)

Square

Can of expanding foam (available in hardware stores)

1/4" (6 mm) staples and staple gun

Spray adhesive

4 square yards (3.6 m) upholstery foam

Electric knife (optional)

Polyester quilt batting, extra thick

3 yards (2.7 m) muslin (scraps are fine)

1

Spread the cardboard out on a flat surface. Draw and cut out the patterns, using the illustration on page 113 as a guide. Feel free to adapt the size or shape if you're trying to match a full-sized sofa.

2

Trace the cardboard patterns onto the plywood and cut out one back piece, one front piece, two side rails, one seat piece, two nailers that look like front arms, and one nailer about 1" wide and the length of the seat. (Note: Making smooth cuts is more important than staying exactly on the lines.)

3

Place the front piece on top of the back piece and trace the outline of the seat. Trim one or both pieces if they are more than 1/4" different in size.

4

Nail and glue the seat nailer below the seat line traced on the front piece. Nail and glue the two arm nailers in place. Nail the side rails in place, nailing through the front side into the side rail and through the back into the side. Nail in both sides.

5

Use a square to double-check that the side pieces are 90 to the back. Place the seat on the seat-support nailer and fasten in place.

6

Cut a length of posterboard the distance from the sofa back to the front, making sure the length is long enough to span from the inside of the arm up and over the bottom of the arm side rail plus a few inches. Cut a notch and slide the posterboard so it slides below the seat. Bend and staple the posterboard to the bottom of the seat. Smooth the posterboard up and over the arms, stapling along the way and cutting notches so it will slide inside the side rail. Staple to the inside of the side rail. Cut off any excess posterboard.

7

Turn the sofa upside down and fill each arm halfway with expanding foam to help stiffen the posterboard. (Overfilling the arms will cause them to bulge out as the foam expands.) Allow the foam to harden overnight.

8

Cut a sheet of upholstery foam to fit the inside back of the couch and secure it in place with spray adhesive. Add a second sheet of foam, starting at the bottom of the seat deck. Taper the second sheet of foam so that it ends up being about half as thick at the top as at the bottom. (Note: If the tapering looks too conspicuous, add a layer or two of batting to smooth it out.)

9

Cover the back with batting, securing with spray adhesive. Add batting from the seat deck up and over the top of the back and down a few inches, then across the arms, starting at the seat deck and working up and across the arms to the bottom of the side rails with a few extra inches hanging over.

10

Trim the overhand flush with the front and back arm faces, then stick a piece of batting onto each arm face and trim it flush with the surrounding batting. Attach a piece of batting from the back of the seat forward and down to the bottom of the front rail.

11

Cover the couch with muslin, working as neatly as possible in the same order as you did the batting and securing in place with staples.

MATERIALS
FOR SLIPCOVER

4 yards (3.6 m) of tightly woven fabric (any decorator fabric is fine, but it should have some give to it)

1 yard (.9 m) scrap fabric

10 yards (9 m) brush fringe or piping (optional but well worth the effort)

Narrow strips of Velcro

2 decorative buttons

*Note: This slipcover was designed and assembled by a professional upholsterer. While the techniques in themselves are not difficult, you may wish to refer to a basic upholstery/slip covering book if you are not familiar with the process.

1

Drape a length of fabric from the top of the inside back down to and across the deck and down to the floor. Cut off the length, leaving allowance for seams and the desired hem depth.

2

Trim the fabric around the inside arm along the deck and at the intersection of the arm and back of the front, leaving flaps on both sides to complete the skirts.

3

Drape the fabric from the deck up and over the inside arm to where the outside arm/side skirt will join. Cut off the excess fabric, allowing for seam allowances and 6" (15 cm) on each side for flaps.

4

Drape the fabric on the outside of the sofa from the cut edge of the inside arm to the floor. Cut off the excess fabric, allowing extra fabric for the hem and seam allowances.

5

Place a scrap piece of fabric onto the arm face, rolling back the edges of the inside/outside arm if necessary. Trim the scrap fabric into the rough shape, adding a seam allowance. Repeat for the other arm, then use the scrap fabric as a pattern to cut out your slipcover fabric.

6

Drape a length of fabric from the top of the outside back to the floor. Cut off the length, leaving enough fabric for desired hem allowance and for a 6" flap on each side. If desired, fold a knife-edge pleat at the center back.

7

Pin the slipcover together along all seams and mark the stitching lines on both sides of each seam. Remove the cover from the sofa. Stitch the outside arm to the inside arm on each side.

8

Remove one arm face. Apply brush fringe and stitch back onto the inside/outside arm section. Repeat on the other side.

9

Stitch the inside arm to the inside back/deck on each side. Remove the outside back from the inside back in the area to have brush fringe. Apply fringe to the inside back, then stitch the outside back to the inside back. Stitch the outside back to the outside arm on each side.

10

Try on the slipcover and make any fitting adjustments. Make a diagonal cut to the stitching at the front inside corner of each arm face/deck seam.

11

Pin and stitch the skirt flaps across the arm faces parallel to the floor. Hem skirts so they fall just above the floor. Lap the side skirt flaps underneath the front skirt and attach. Repeat with back skirt flaps.

12

Slip the cover onto the sofa and mark the button placements. Remove the cover and stitch Velcro inside the pleat at the button placements. Secure the Velcro together and fluff the fringe.

MATERIALS
FOR SEAT CUSHION

Pillow form to fit seating area

Leftover fabric from slip cover

2 yards (1.8 m) fringe

Zipper

1

Measure the length and width of the pillow form seam to seam. Cut two rectangles of fabric 2" (5 cm) larger in each direction.

2

On one of the rectangles, fold the raw edges of each corner over to create a diagonal fold and pin. Place this rectangle over the pillow form and adjust the pins so that the cover fits without being too snug or too loose.

3

Remove the rectangle from the form and equalize the pins so that the fold happens at the same distance from each point. Fold and pin the other rectangle to match.

4

Apply brush fringe to the short sides and one long edge of one rectangle. Place the rectangles with right sides facing and pin along the unfringed edge.

5

Starting on a short side 1" (2.5 cm) from the unfringed corner, stitch to the corner. Baste along the edge, and stitch around corner 1".

6

Press open. Apply a zipper to the basted seam. Remove basting. Open zipper 4" (10 cm). With right sides together, pin and stitch the three sides to close the pillow cover.

7

Turn the pillow cover right sides out through the zipper. Place it over the form and fluff the fringe.

DESIGN
LEAH NALL & CARL THOMAS

Scratch Post Play Arrangement

MATERIALS

- 22" (55 cm) or taller basket
- 5' (1.6 m) 1/4" (6 mm) sisal rope
- Stalks of playful grasses (uva, wheat, formosa, and red-tip grass were used here)
- Focal bloom (cardone puffs were used here)
- 1 stem of curly vine
- Stones
- Spanish moss
- Floral foam, pins, and picks
- 18-gauge stub wires
- Plastic golf ball
- Catnip and catnip mouse

1

Place the rope in a box and sprinkle catnip over it. Cover the box and let stand for several days. Remove the rope and rub crumbled catnip onto it. Attach the rope to an area of the basket easy for the cat to reach for scratching. The rope can be attached to the basket with a glue gun or it can be woven into the basket.

2

Weight the bottom of the basket with stones, then fill it with crumpled newspaper to about 6" (15 cm) from the top of the basket. Cut a piece of floral foam to fit snugly in the remaining 6". Cover the foam with Spanish moss and secure the moss with floral pins.

3

Begin inserting stems of dried materials into the foam, positioning some of the materials low enough for the cat to play with. Thin, delicate stems, such as wheat, should be reinforced before inserting into the foam to prevent breakage. To reinforce a stem, place a floral pick about 2" (5 cm) away from the bottom of a stem or grouping of stems. Make several loops with the attached wire to secure, then spiral the wire down the stem(s).

4

Hot-glue a length of curly vine into the foam on one side of the basket, then hot-glue a catnip mouse onto the vine. For a extra playful touch, push one end of a 12" (30 cm) length of rope through a hole in a golf ball. Pull out 1/4" (6 mm) of the rope, squirt on a large glob of hot glue, and pull it back into the ball. Tie the rope onto the basket.

DESIGN
KIT MECKLEY

Worth Pondering ...

News reports are often filled with wondrous and entertaining notes about our interactions with cats, yet there's a sad side to the story as well.

According to the National Humane Society, an estimated 7.5 million cats and dogs are unable to find homes, and on average 80% of the animals taken it at shelters are euthanized.

In seven years, an unsterilized female cat and her offspring can produce approximately 420,000 cats.

Never underestimate the benefits of identification tags. American Humane Association studies reveal that only 3 of 100 tagless cats brought to shelters are ever reunited with their families.

Cats run the risk of accidental poisoning just as children do. To protect you feline, store all medicines, cleaning supplies, and chemicals out of your cat's reach. Read the labels of antifreeze products for "pet safe" varieties. Never medicate your cat without consulting your vet. Even simple medicines like aspirin can be poisonous. Make a list of plants in and around your home and take it with you on your next vet visit. More than 150 plants can be poisonous to your cat.

Floor Cloth

MATERIALS

Heavy artist's canvas

Gesso

Paintbrushes

Sandpaper

Push pins

Peel-away tape

Rubber contact cement

Polymer or acrylic paints

**Foam-block prints or
  sponges, optional**

Clear, water-based sealer

1

Cut and tape several sheets of newspaper to the desired size of your floor cloth plus 3 to 4" (7.5 - 10 cm) on all sides. Use the newspaper to plan your design and as a pattern to cut out your canvas. Stretch the canvas over a large, flat surface (a sheet of plywood is ideal) and push-pin the edges in place.

2

Apply a coat of gesso to the canvas and allow it to dry. Tape a piece of sandpaper over a small wooden block and sand the gessoed surface. Towel off the dust, then gesso and sand twice more. Repeat on the back side if a two-sided floor cloth is desired.

3

Trim off any excess canvas, leaving 1" (2.5 cm) on all

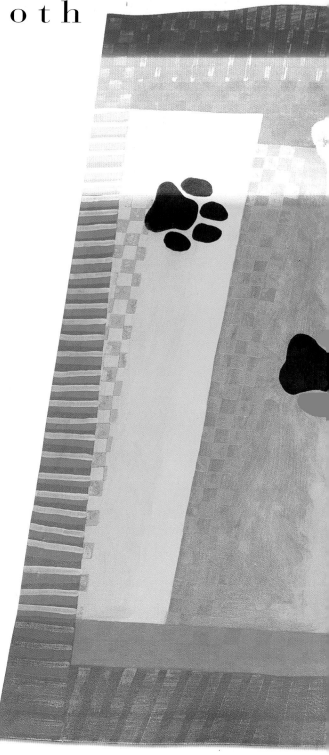

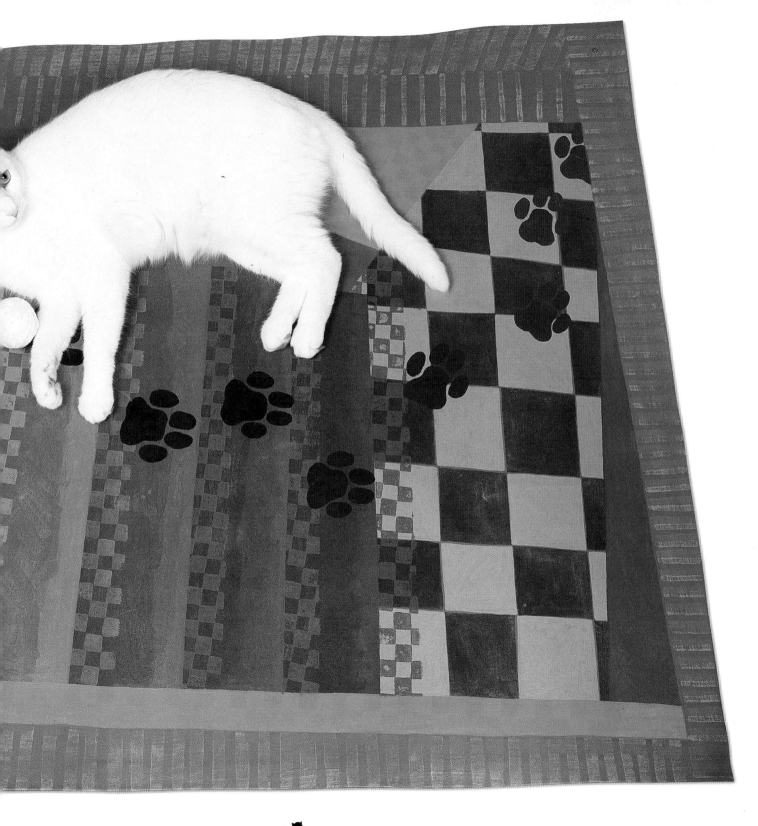

DESIGN
HEATHER ALLEN

45

sides for a hem. Working on one side at a time, fold down an edge and press it down with the back of a butter knife. Repeat on all sides, mitering the corners. Secure with contact cement and clamp with weights until the cement is completely dry.

+

Apply in pencil the design you plan to paint, then begin working with paints. (See page 110 for paw print stencil.) For this design, the artist created stencils on the canvas with peel-away tape and then sponged the areas inside the stencil to create a padlike effect.

5

When the paint is completely dry, apply three coats of sealer, allowing each coat to completely dry before adding the next. Note: Test for dryness by lightly touching the canvas. A cool feel means there is still moisture in the paint and the cloth needs additional drying time.

DESIGN
HEATHER ALLEN

Kitty Stationery

MATERIALS

Watercolor or handmade
 paper and matching
 envelopes
Watercolor paints and
 brush and/or puff paints
Craft knife
Paper towels and/or
 kitchen sponge

1

Trim your paper down to a size you like and cut a paw print stencil with a craft knife from the pattern on page 110.

2

Position the stencil patterns on the paper so the paws appear to be walking across the paper. Note that partial prints often create the most dramatic effects. Dab the paint into the stencil area with a crumpled paper towel or kitchen sponge.

3

For interesting variations, try tracing a second paw print 1/2" (12 mm) up from the first one to create a shadowed effect; or, try overlapping paw prints on top of each other and outlining their shapes with contrasting colors of puff paint.

SHADOW CAT MOTIFS

MATERIALS

Watercolor and/or hand-made paper and matching envelopes
Craft knife
#2 or softer pencil
Sheet of white typing paper
Watercolor paints

1

Trim your paper down to a size you like. Choose one of the images on page 126 and photocopy it. Tape the image down on a flat surface and tape the white piece of paper over it. Outline the white areas and fill them in with a heavy layer of pencil.

2

Turn the white paper over and position it on top of your paper. Remove the blade from your craft knife and rub the back side of the paper firmly with the bottom of the knife. Double-check that the image has completely transferred before lifting the paper.

3

Fill in the space around the pencil with a solid coat of paint. After the paint has completely dried, carefully erase the penciled image.

FAUX WAX SEAL

MATERIALS

Envelopes
Gold or silver puff paint

1

Adjust the size of the motif on page 126 to a size you like and cut a stencil from it. Transfer the motif with light pencil marks.

2

Address the front of the envelope, insert the letter, and seal shut. Fill in the paw print motif with a thick layer of puff paint.

DESIGN
CAROLINE QUEEN OTTINGER

Cat Paws

Felines are the original toe dancers, their telltale footprints serving as both revered and despised calling cards. The forefeet have five toes, while the hind feet have four. Thick, tough pads protect the toes and serve as shock absorbers. The pads also have sweat glands, so don't be surprised if paw prints suddenly show up on a hot day or in the vet's office. Claws, which protrude from the tips of the pads, are used for traction and digging, as well as self-defense.

Cats bearing extra toes are often referred to as Hemingway cats, named for a six-toed cat given to well-known author Ernest Hemingway by a boat captain. (Extra toes, also known as polydactylism, is a dominate genetic trait, so one multitoed cat soon breeds another.) Years ago, polydactyl cats were considered good luck by sailors, and often traveled with them on ships. In Europe, polydactyl cats are far less common because their unusual feet were considered a sign of witchcraft during medieval times and the cats were killed.

Ernest Hemingway with one of his polydactyl cats, circa 1950s. Photo courtesy John Fitzgerald Kennedy Library and Look Magazine.

Paper Kittens

MATERIALS

Large sheet of handmade paper in a neutral color

Clear gloss medium and brush

Liquid fabric dye and spray bottle

Puff paints

Foam core (for clock and wall hanging)

Craft glue

Clock mechanism (for clock)

Hanging hook (for clock and wall hanging)

1

Enlarge one of the cat motifs on page 116, trace it onto the paper, and cut it out. For a switchplate cover, cut the cat just a little larger than the plate.

2

Mix some liquid dye in a plastic spray bottle and spritz it onto the paper in light coats, varying the intensity of the color as you work. Add additional colors in the same manner, allowing each coat to completely dry before adding the next.

3

Strengthen and seal the paper by brushing on several layers of clear gloss medium, allowing each coat to dry before adding the next. Add features and patterns with puff paint.

4

For the switchplate covers, glue the paper directly to the plate. For the clocks and wall pieces, cut out a piece of foam core in the same shape but slightly smaller. Glue the foam core to the back of the paper. Glue a hanging hook onto the back of the wall piece. For the clock, attach the clock arms on the front side and the battery mechanism and a hanging hook on the back side.

Note: For alternate motifs, search out simple cat designs in children's books or advertisements. Blow them up with an enlarging copying machine and use their basic shape as a pattern.

DESIGN
CLAUDIA LEE

Sweet Kitty

MATERIALS

*Package of instant paper
  mache*
Small paper plate
Sculpting or manicure tools
Acrylic paints
Antiquing medium
White craft glue
Small silk flower
**15" (37 cm) length of 1/2"
(12 mm) wide lace trim**
**10" (25 cm) length of 1/8"
(3 mm) wide ribbon**

1

Mix the paper mache according to the manufacturer's instructions. Form the paper plate into a cone that is 5" (13 cm) tall and 2-1/2" (6 cm) wide at the base. Secure it together with tape.

2

Make a 1" (2.5 cm) ball of mache and press it into the top of the cone to form a rough head shape. Cover the cone with a 1/2" layer of mache. Press fabric folds into the mache with the tools. Allow to completely dry.

3

Roll out two coils of paper mache for arms and press them in place, bending at the elbows. Form two small balls of mache into balls and press them into the end of the coils to form paws. Press creases into the sleeves and indents into the paws with the tools.

4

Roll out a short, narrow coil for the tail and press it into the bottom of the skirt. Press a small ball of mache against the opposite side of the skirt and press paw grooves in place.

5

Roll out a 1/2" thick layer of mache and cut an oval shape out of it for the hat and press it in place. Add small pieces of mache to form the ears, cheeks, and muzzle. Blend in and add details with the tools. Allow to completely dry.

6

Glue on the lace, ribbon, and silk flower trims. For a porcelainlike finish, mix equal parts of water and white glue and brush on three coats, allowing each coat to completely dry before adding the next.

DESIGN
DOLLY LUTZ

Sticker Art

Frame and mat board set

*Colorful assortment of cat
stickers, old decals, or
magazine photos*

*Antique photograph or
postcard with humorous
theme*

Craft glue

Stars, optional

1

Position and affix the photograph or postcard in the
center of the mat board.
Arrange the stickers in the
remaining space and glue in
place. Finish with colorful
stars if desired.

*Note: The same techniques
can be applied to create a
gift for a child's room. Look
for nursery rhyme stickers
and postcards with themes
such as The Cat and the
Fiddle, Puss 'n Boots, The
Three Little Kittens, etc.*

DESIGN
LEAH BECKWITH

53

MATERIALS

15 x 20" (37 x 50 cm) piece of 1/4" (6 mm) plywood
Acrylic paints and brushes
Exterior grade varnish

1

Mark off a border design in pencil. Paint the outside of the border in dark blue, then paint the area inside the border sky blue.

2

Working with the motifs on page 118 or from your own, position and outline the details with pencil. Paint as desired.

3

After the paint has completely dried, finish with two coats of varnish. Mount on a wooden stake or hang with hooks and a chain.

DESIGN
DOLLY LUTZ MORRIS

Cat Crossing

MATERIALS

*11" (27 cm) diameter circle
of 1/4" (6 mm) plywood*

Sand paper

*Set of 1" (2.5 cm) and 3/4"
(18 mm) letter stencils*

Acrylic paints and brushes

Exterior-grade varnish

Sandpaper

1

Sand the edges of the plywood circle. Apply two base
coats of yellow paint and let
dry.

2

Position the letter stencils on
the circle, using 1" stencils
for the word "cat" and 3/4"
stencils for the word "cross-
ing." Outline the stencils in
pencil.

3

Enlarge the cat pattern on
page 122. Position the stencils as desired and outline
in pencil. Paint the letters
and cats with black paint
and allow to completely dry.

4

Finish with two coats of
varnish, then hang with
hooks and a chain or mount
on a wooden stake.

DESIGN
JUDITH STOLL, DOLLY LUTZ MORRIS

Betsy Cat and Sailor Cat

MATERIALS

Package of instant paper mache

3" (7.5 cm) foam ball

Sculpting or manicure tools

Acrylic paints and brushes

Antiquing medium

Spray polyurethane

Flag paper ribbon, needle, red sewing thread, and a short length of narrow lace (for Betsy)

1

Mix the paper mache according to the manufacturer's instructions. Cover the foam ball with a 1/2" (12 mm) thick layer of mache. At the top, add a 1-1/2" (4 cm) ball of mache to create a rough head shape. Allow the mache to completely dry.

2

Roll out two coils of mache that are 1-3/4" (5 cm) thick and 4" (10 cm) long for the arms. Press the coils in place, bending them at the elbows. Add 1/2" balls for paws.

3

Roll out a 1/2" thick layer of mache. Cut out the head area and taper the front section to form collars. Form bows and ties and press in place.

4

Add small bits of mache to form cheeks, a muzzle, and ears, using tools to shape and form. Cut out a 3/4" (18 mm) thick circle of mache to form a hat. Shape and press in place. For Betsy Cat, dip a narrow length of lace in white glue or fabric stiffener and shape it around the hat. Allow the mache to completely dry.

5

Paint, seal, antique, and seal again, allowing each coat to completely dry before adding the next. After the last sealant coat dries, glue a short length of flag ribbon between Betsy's paws. Thread a sewing needle and glue it behind the ribbon. Coat the ribbon with white craft glue and curve it around one paw.

DESIGN
DOLLY LUTZ MORRIS

Kitty Frame

MATERIALS

Wooden photo frame

Painted cat wood cutout (purchased in a craft store)

Four colors of craft paint

Paintbrush

Several 1/2 to 3/4" (12 - 18 mm) diameter wood balls with a flat side (purchased in a craft store)

1 yard (.9 m) each of silk cording to match three of the paint colors

1

Paint the frame in a background color. After the paint dries, position and hot-glue the cat cutout on one corner of the frame. Paint the balls in the three remaining paint colors.

2

Wrap the balls in a coordinating color of silk cording, leaving a 12" (30 cm) tail and dabbing the underside of the ball as needed with hot glue to prevent the cording from unraveling.

3

Position and hot-glue the flat side of the balls against the frame, then twist and tangle the cording tails up and around the frame. Tuck the cording under the cat's paw, glue in place, and trim off any excess.

DESIGN
KIM TIBBALS-THOMPSON

MATERIALS

1 package polymer clay

Toothpick

2 beads for eyes

Colored wire or stiff hair

1/4 yard (.2 m) metallic "eyelash fabric"

Stuffing

Craft glue

Blue acrylic paint and brush

1

Flatten a 1" (2.5 cm) round ball of clay into a 1/4" (6 mm) thick disk. Apply a small length of clay in the center to form the nose. Apply two clay disks to form the cheeks.

2

Blend the clay in to create features. Sculpt eyes with a toothpick and place a bead in the center. Bake according to the manufacturer's instructions. Glue wire or stiff hair in place for whiskers.

3

Cut out the cat pattern on page 119 from doubled fabric. Pin with right sides together and sew with a narrow seam allowance, leaving a 3" (7.5 cm) opening for turning. Turn right sides out and stuff, then slip stitch the opening closed.

4

Cut a circle slightly smaller than the head size in the fabric. Slip the head inside and glue in place. Paint the cat with blue acrylic paint.

MATERIALS

1/4 yard (.2 m) colorful
fabric

Craft or telephone wire, cut
in 4" (10 cm) lengths

Stuffing

Cotton balls

Wheat paste

1

Cut out the pattern on page 121 from a doubled layer of fabric. Pierce the pattern piece with a length of 4" wire as if it were a needle, making a stitch so the ends of the wire are on the top. Twist the wire to keep in place. Repeat with additional lengths of wire until the body is covered with wire hair.

2

Keeping the wire side up, sew the top to the bottom, leaving a 3" (7.5 cm) opening for stuffing. Stuff the cat well, then slip-stitch the opening closed.

3

Soak three cotton balls in wheat paste and sculpt a nose and cheeks from them. Press the balls onto the fabric surface. Dip small pieces of newspaper in the wheat paste and use them to cover the cotton ball base and to flesh out facial details.

4

Press beads in the eye area and allow the mache to completely dry. Add a second layer of newspaper pieces to fill out the face and allow to completely dry. Paint the cat's face to match the body.

MATERIALS

1/4 yard (.2 m) cotton fabric

Stuffing

Quilting thread

Seed beads

1 package polymer clay

Craft glue

Toothpick

1

Cut out the cat pattern on page 120 from doubled fabric. Sew the cat with wrong sides facing, leaving a 3" (7.5 cm) opening for stuffing. Stuff the cat (do not reverse the cat) and slip stitch the opening shut.

2

Thread a needle with a length of quilting thread and pull it through the fabric until 1-1/2" (4 cm) of thread remains. Tie two knots, add a bead, tie again, and cut the thread. Repeat until you've created a textured surface on the entire body.

3

Flatten a 1" (2.5 cm) round ball of clay into a 1/4" (6 mm) thick disk. Apply a small length of clay in the center to form the nose. Apply two clay disks to form the cheeks.

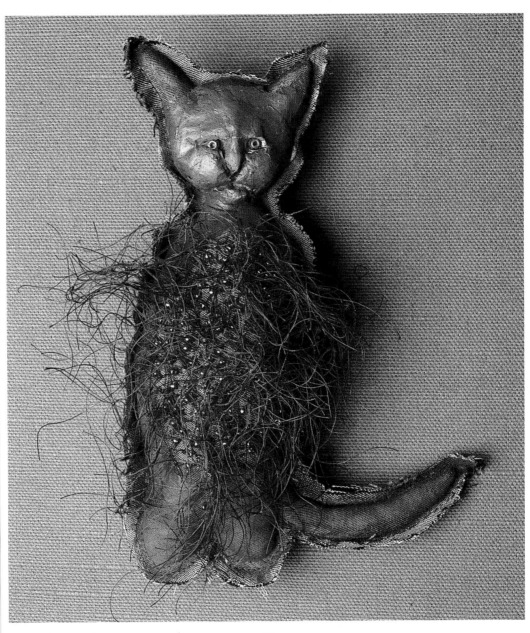

4

Blend the clay to create feline features. Sculpt eyes with a toothpick and place a bead in the center. Bake according to the manufacturer's instructions. Glue wire or stiff hair in place for whiskers.

5

Cut a circle in the fabric slightly smaller than the head size. Slip the head inside and glue in place.

DESIGN
BRENNA BUSSE

61

Needlepoint Felines

MATERIALS

7-mesh needlepoint canvas cut 2" (5 cm) larger on all sides than the finished size

2 #18 tapestry needles

Paternayan Persian tapestry wool

Batting or other stuffing

1/4 yard (.2 m) velveteen or upholstery-weight fabric

Decorative braiding, optional

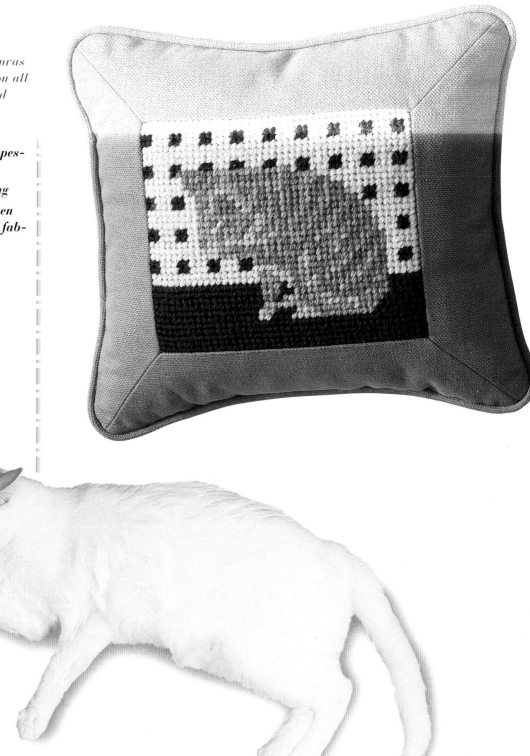

62

1

Cut a piece of 7-mesh canvas to the size of the finished design plus 2" on all sides. Separate the three-ply wool into individual strands and thread your needle with four strands.

2

Stitch the designs in a continental or basketweave stitch, working on the details first and then the outside border. Whenever possible, work the lightest colors first to avoid catching darker colored threads in the lighter colors. Each square on the chart represents one stitch and the symbol inside each square indicates the yarn color. As you come to the end of each strand of wool, gently run it through the back of 7 to 10 stitches. Avoid jumping the wool from one area of color to another unless they are within 5 or 6 stitches in any direction.

3

Block your finished piece if necessary. To make an 8" (20 cm) pillow, cut and sew 3" (7.5 cm) fabric strips to all four sides of the design and then miter the corners, stitching between the first and second row of the needlepoint. Use the bordered needlepoint piece as a pattern to cut a piece of backing fabric. Stitch the two pieces together with right sides facing, leaving a 4" (10 cm) opening for turning. Turn the fabric right sides out, stuff it with batting, and slip stitch the opening closed. Note: decorative braiding sewn into the seam creates a more finished look.

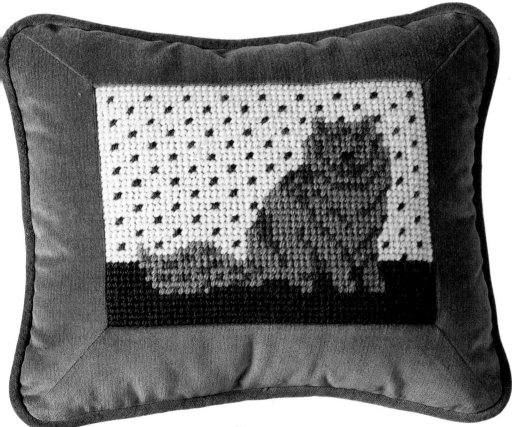

DESIGN
CATHERINE REURS

STITCHING
MARY ANN PARKER

ORANGE TABBY CAT: Finished size 6" wide x 5" high (15 x 13 cm)

Color	Color #	Amount of Wool 4-ply 32" (80 cm) strands
White bkgrd	#263	12 strands
Blue bkgrd	#500	12 strands
Light orange	#499	4 strands
Med. orange	#497	7 strands
Dark orange	#496	7 strands

GREY PERSIAN CAT: Finished size 8" wide x 6" high (20 x 15 cm)

Color	Color #	Amount of Wool (4-ply strands)
White bkgrd	#263	22 strands
Green bkgrd	#690	15 strands
Light grey	#202	10 strands
Med. grey	#200	7 strands
Dark Grey (eye)	#221	1 strand
Orange (eye)	#497	1 strand

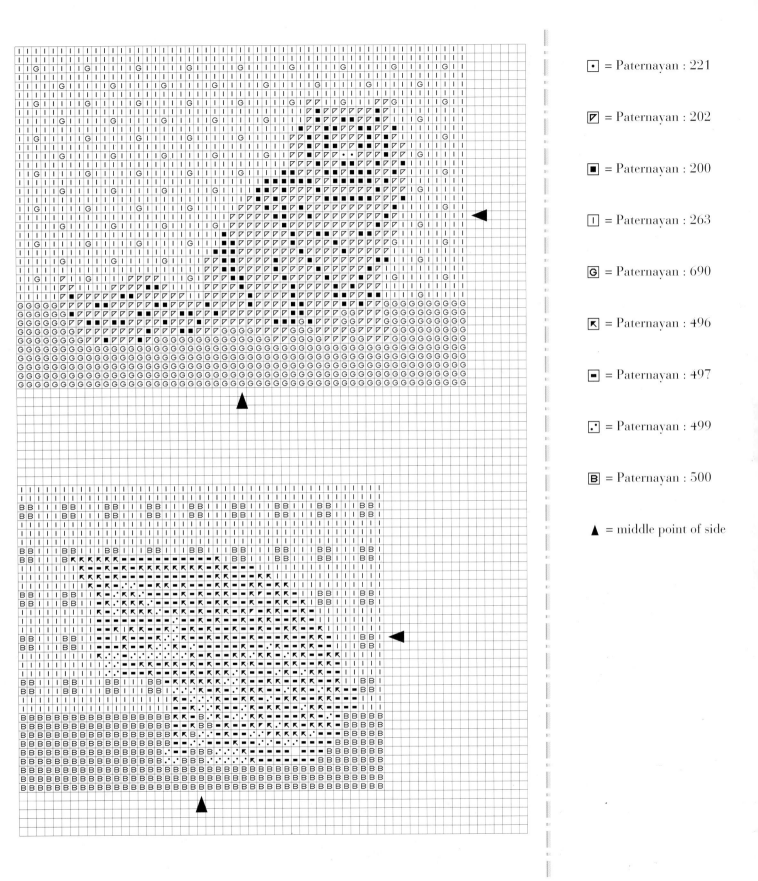

- ⊡ = Paternayan : 221
- ⊽ = Paternayan : 202
- ▪ = Paternayan : 200
- ⊡ = Paternayan : 263
- Ⓖ = Paternayan : 690
- Ⓚ = Paternayan : 496
- ⊟ = Paternayan : 497
- ⊡ = Paternayan : 499
- Ⓑ = Paternayan : 500
- ▲ = middle point of side

Playful Cats Shade

MATERIALS

Old paper lamp shade

Fine sandpaper

Lamp shade paper and lining paper in a neutral color

2 lengths of contrasting trim, one 5/8" (15 mm) wide cotton grosgrain, one narrow silk cording

Paper piercer (available in larger craft stores)

Safety glasses

Craft knife with extra blades

Clear-drying craft glue

Acrylic or watercolor paints and brushes

Sheet of framing glass

Bulldog clips

Fishing weights

1

Carefully remove the paper from an old lamp shade and press it flat with an iron. Lightly sand the frame or top and bottom rings to remove any excess glue and set aside. Save the frame or the top and bottom rings. Use the paper as a pattern to cut out the outer and liner shade papers.

2

Lightly transfer the kitty motifs on page 106 around the lower edge of the back side of your paper. Prepare a work surface by folding a terry-cloth towel in half and placing the paper on top of it with its right side facing down.

3

Outline the yarn with a piercer in 1/8" (3 mm) intervals using a small needle. The needle should bounce easily out from the paper, creating a candlewicked appearance on the right side of the paper. Add facial details and fur stripes with the piercer in 1/16" (1.5 mm) intervals.

4

Tape the edges of a sheet of framing glass and place the paper on it with its right side facing down. Begin the cutwork with a craft knife and a fine, sharp blade. (Wear your safety glasses!) The goal is to make smooth, even cuts without jerking. The heavy lines on the pattern are cut lines. Fix any small tears with a clear-drying craft glue.

5

Paint the kitties, taking care to keep excess water off the paper to prevent buckling. Gently erase all pencil marks.

6

Mark the bottom center of your paper with a light pencil mark. Position it on the bottom shade ring and fasten the edge with a bulldog clip at a 45-degree angle. Working toward the left, continue fitting and clipping the paper until you reach the end of the paper.

7

Return to the center front and repeat in the other direction. Overlap the back seam left over right when you reach the end and fasten with a bulldog clip. Carefully look for and fix any gaps, then stand the shade upright with the center front facing you.

8

Fit the paper to the top ring as you did the bottom. Release the bulldog clips on both sides of the seam and glue the seam together. Remove the remaining clips and wipe off any excess glue with a clean cloth. Press weights along the inside of the back seam to ensure flat, even drying.

9

Position and glue the shade to the frame or to the top and bottom rings, securing in place with clips until dry. Working in 10" (25 cm) increments, apply glue to the lower half of the binding. Position and fingerpress the binding around the shade. Add glue to the bottom half, fold it around the shade, and fingerpress in place, cutting grooves in the binding if necessary to fit around the top fixture. Crease the edge of the binding and remove any excess glue. Brush on a light coat of glue at the top edge of the wide binding and press the cording in place.

Note: Display with a low-wattage bulb.

> "OUTSIDE OF A CAT, A BOOK IS MAN'S BEST FRIEND. INSIDE OF A CAT, IT'S TOO DARK TO READ."
> — ROBERT ERICSON

DESIGN
CHRIS NOAH-COOPER

Santa Cat

Package of instant paper mache

Sculpting or manicure tools

5" (13 cm) length of 1/8" (3 mm) wide ribbon

10" (25 cm) length of 1-1/2" (4 cm) wide ribbon

2" (5 cm) tall artificial tree

Small bell

7" (18 cm) length of beaded garland

Acrylic paints and small brush

Antiquing medium

Spray polyurethane

Large paper plate

Sheet of cardboard

1

Mix the paper mache according to the manufacturer's instructions. Fold the paper plate into a 10" high cone with a 5" wide base and tape it together. Cover the cone with a 1/2" (12 mm) thick layer of paper mache. Add a 2" ball of paper mache at the top for the rough head form. Allow the mache to completely dry.

2

Roll out two coils for the front legs and press them in place. Press small balls of mache into the base of each leg for paws. Roll out a 1" (2.5 cm) thick piece of mache and cut two ovals for back haunches. Press the haunches in place, then press small balls of mache into the haunches for back paws.

3

Shape the newly added mache and blend it in with the tools, pressing in vertical lines for paws. Add a curving tail with a long coil of mache.

4

Crumple a small piece of newspaper into a rough bag shape and cover it with mache mixture. Press the bag against one side of the body so that it rests on one haunch. Roll a out long coil of mache and work it around the opposite shoulder to form a strap. Form a small mouse head and press it into the top of the bag.

5

Shape, mold, and blend the facial features using tools. Build up the shoulders with additional paper mache. Shape a hat and press in place, pressing small grooves into the trim areas until it resembles fur. Allow the mache to completely dry.

6

Paint the cat as desired, then seal, antique, and seal again, allowing each coat to completely dry before adding the next and referring to the manufacturer's instructions. Allow the final sealant coat to completely dry.

7

Glue the wide ribbon around the cat's neck and tie in a bow. Repeat with the narrow ribbon and the mouse. Coat the ribbons with a light layer of craft glue to stiffen. Hot-glue the bell, beads, tree, and small ball of yarn in the bag, allowing a short length of the yarn to hang down. Stiffen the yarn by coating it with craft glue and shape it down the cat's body.

> "**THE DOG GIVES HIMSELF THE AIRS OF A CAT.**"
> — RICHARD STEELE

Garden Wire Cats

*36" (.9 m) length of heavy
electrical or phone wire in
the color of your choice*
**(available by the foot in
hardware stores)**
Soft-nosed pliers

1

Using one of the cat motifs
on pages 103 - 126 as a
guide, begin shaping the
wire to form an outline of
the motif, beginning about
8" (20 cm) up from the
wire's end.

2

As you reach the end of the
motif, twist the wire down
your beginning 8". Cut off
any excess wire and bury at
least 6" (15 cm) of the bottom wire in the ground.

*Note: Smaller cats can be
formed with thinner gauges
of wire and spraypainted
with metallic colors for simple, festive tree ornaments
and package decorations.*

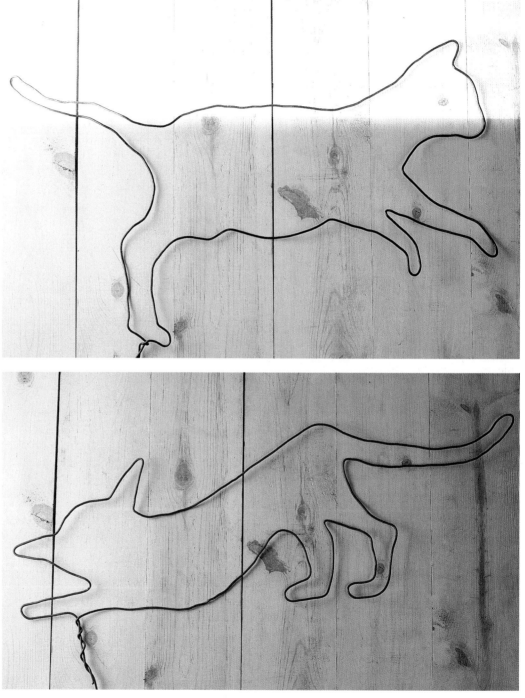

DESIGN
CAROLINE OTTINGER

70

Arresting Spritz Bottles

Metal or plastic spritz bottle

One or more colors of puff paint

1

Transfer the motif on page 124 onto the spritz bottle. Outline the pattern with one or more colors of puff paint. After the paint completely dries, fill the bottle with water

2

Place the bottle near the couch or other area where kitty tends to get into trouble. Spritz kitty lightly during the offending action.

DESIGN
CAROLINE OTTINGER

How Do They Do That?

How do cats see in the dark? Although cats can make out more detail and movement in dark areas than humans, they cannot see in pitch darkness. Cats have a light-reflecting layer of tissue in the back of their eyes that allows them to utilize every bit of available light, allowing them to see objects invisible to us.

How do cats always manage to land on their feet? An instinctive "righting reflex" helps a falling cat reorient itself in the air. First the head rotates upright, then the front legs come close to the face, then the upper spine twists, bringing the front half of the body in line with the head, and finally the hind legs bend up. The tail remains stiff and acts as a counterbalance.

How are cats able to pick out the lone cat hater in a room full of cat lovers? No, cats are not psychic, their senses just seem to be better tuned than ours. What probably happens, researchers speculate, is that all of the cat lovers are looking at the cat, cooing at it, maybe even beckoning it to come their way. Instead, the cat goes for the person who seems the calmest and least threatening — the person who is ignoring him.

How do cats manage to keep their balance so well? The cat's remarkable balancing skills can be credited to the incredible speed at which the messages sent from the eyes and inner ears reach the muscles. A cat walking along a narrow ledge may "almost fall" several times a minute, but she's able to make remarkably quick balance adjustments. A cat's tail also contributes to its fine balance, serving as both a counter-balance and a counterweight as the situation warrants.

Cat Tail Rack

MATERIALS

18 x 18" (46 cm) poster-board

3/4" plywood (8 x 19", 20 x 48 cm, for base; 15 x 17", 38 x 43 cm, for body; 12 x 14", 31 x 36 cm, for tail; and 3-1/2 x 5", 9 x 13 cm, for brace)

1 x 15" (2.5 x 38 cm) dowel

Sandpaper

Wood filler

#6 x 1-5/8" (4 cm) decking screws

Acrylic paints and brushes

Polyurethane finish

TOOLS

Jigsaw (band saw or scroll saw)

Router (optional)

Drill and bits (1/8" and 3/8", 3 mm and 9 mm)

1

Enlarge the design on page 105 and transfer it onto the posterboard. Cut out the posterboard and use it as a pattern to cut out the ply-wood.

2

Cut out all pieces, then rout or sand the edges. Drill and countersink all holes. Mount the brace to the body and fill the holes with wood filler.

3

Paint all pieces and allow to completely dry, then finish with several coats of a clear finish.

4

Screw the body/brace to the base from the bottom. Screw the tail to the body from the back. Screw the dowel to the base from the bottom.

DESIGN
NORRIS HALL

Shadow Puppets

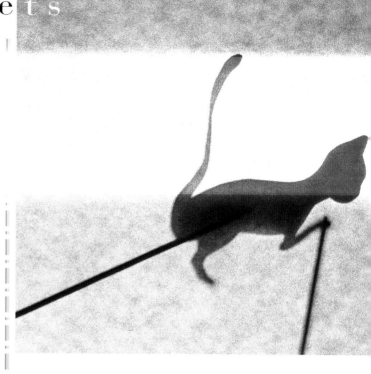

80 lb. card stock

Craft knife

*Nylon thread and sewing
needle*

Strong, clear-drying glue

Small carving tool

Wooden cooking skewers

1

Trace the motifs on page 117 onto the card stock and cut them out with a sharp craft knife.

2

Position the hinged pieces as desired. Thread the nylon onto a needle and tie a knot on the other end. Pull the thread through the center of the hinge. Place a drop of glue on top of the knot, make a stitch, and finish with a knot on the other side. Place a drop of glue on top of the second knot.

3

To attach the skewers to the hinged areas, carve a small ridge (just wide enough for the thread) about 1/8" (3 mm) down from the pointed edge. Stitch through the paper where you want the skewer to attach and wrap the thread around the ridge several times. Go back through the paper, make a knot, and put a dab of glue on top of the knot. To attach the main holding stick, carve ridges 1/8" and 3/4" (18 mm) down from the pointed end of a skewer. Attach the threads as directed above.

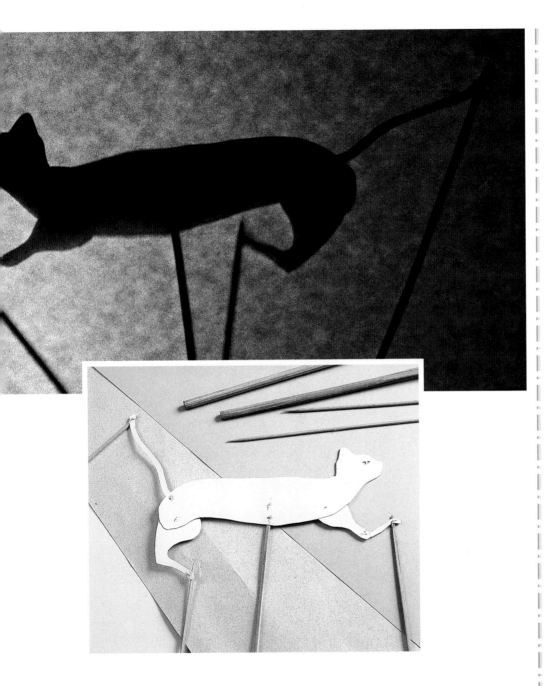

Crafty Cats

So your feline wants to take up knitting . . . "Anatomically impossible," says veterinarian Dr. Rob Rankin. "Unlike humans, cats do not have opposable thumbs, so they cannot grasp and manipulate objects like knitting needles." What about sponge painting? "Definitely a possibility," says Dr. Rankin, "but be sure to choose a water-based paint and carefully wash your cat's paw pads when finished." Any chance for woodworking? "No way," says Dr. Rankin, "and it's definitely not safe to let your cat watch you in the shop either. Their eyes are very vulnerable to flying debris, and most hardware stores do not carry a good selection of feline safety goggles." What about tin punching or cross-stitch? "We're back to the opposable thumb problem again," says Dr. Rankin with a shake of the head. "But most cats are eager to watch you crafting, and even more thrilled to sit in the middle of a project."

DESIGN
KIMBERLY SHUCK

Cattin' Around

Cat Pins

MATERIALS

Sheet of heavy watercolor paper

Craft knife

Watercolor paints with metallic and pearlescent pigments added or any combination of puff paints, fabric paints, markers, and glitter glue

Small brushes

Clear aerosol sealant or acrylic varnish

Craft glue

Pin backings

1

Trace the motifs on page 111 onto the back side of the watercolor paper. Cut them out with a craft knife.

2

Cover each cat with a background coat of paint. Add swirls and features with contrasting colors of metallic pigments, puff paints, markers, or glitter glue. Allow the paints to completely dry.

3

Finish the cats with a coat of aerosol sealant or varnish. After the sealant has completely dried, glue a pin backing to the back of the cat.

DESIGN
MARY MARTIN

Cat Resist Scarf

MATERIALS

Silk scarf in neutral color (blank scarves can be purchased inexpensively in larger craft stores)

*Resist (hot wax, gutta, etc: **Tulip Paper Paint in cranberry was used here**)*

Silk fabric dyes in grey and a range of graduated colors

1" (2.5 cm) foam brushes

1

Enlarge the motifs on pages 107 and 110 to the desired size and transfer them to the right side of the scarf. (With some silks, you may be able to place the silk on top of the motifs and just trace over them.)

2

Fill in the paw prints and outline the cat with resist. (Resists keeps the area where the paint is applied from absorbing dye.)

3

Mix the silk dyes as directed in the manufacturer's instructions. Brush the grey dye inside the resist lines, then brush on graduated colors of dye in the background.

4

Send the scarf to the dry cleaner to remove the resist.

Note: The basic techniques of silk painting can be mastered in a weekend, while the subtleties of the craft can take a lifetime to master. Purchase several extra blank scarves and do not be afraid to experiment.

DESIGN
BETTY
KERSHNER

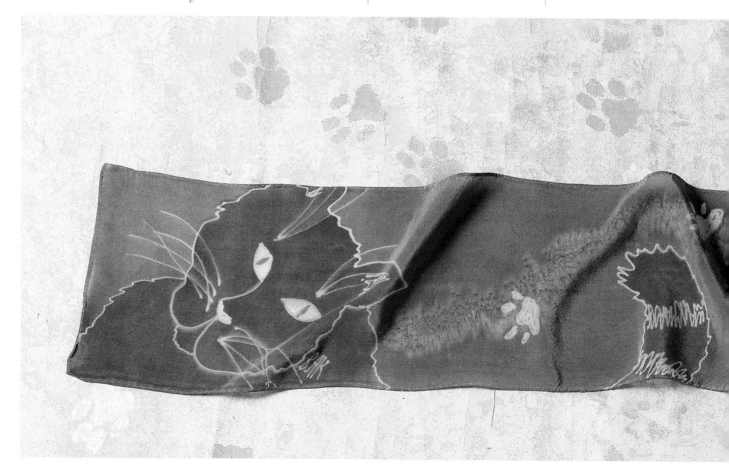

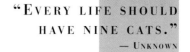

Neck Wear

VICTORIAN RUFFLE

MATERIALS

1 yard (.9 m) 3" (7.5 cm) flat lace

1 yard 6" (15 cm) nylon tulle

3/8 yard (.3 m) white double-fold bias tape

3/8 yard 1/4" (6 mm) double-faced satin ribbon

1

Measure the distance around your cat's neck and add 2" (5 cm) for ease and folding hems. Fold the tulle in half and baste the raw edge of the tulle to the wrong side of the lace.

2

Machine- or hand-gather the top edge of the lace and gather to the desired length. Finish each short edge by folding the lace and tulle down about 1/4" and stitching.

3

Apply binding to the top edge, leaving a 1-1/2" (4 cm) tail on each end. Fold each tail over 1/4" and then stitch it to the neckline, creating a loop.

4

Bring the ribbon through both loops and tie into a bow. Tack one side of the ribbon to the loop to prevent it from slipping out during tying.

SAILOR COLLAR

MATERIALS

1/4 yard (.2 m) blue broadcloth

5/8 yard (.7 m) white braid

1 yard (.9 m) red double-fold bias tape

1

Cut out the collar pattern on page 110 from doubled fabric. Sew the braid 3/4" (18 mm) in from the raw edges along the sides of one collar piece, going all the way to the edges. Repeat along the back edge.

2

Stitch the two collars together with a 1/4" (6 mm) seam allowance with right sides facing, leaving the neck curve open. Turn right sides out and press.

3

Finish one end of the bias tape by folding in the raw edges and stitching them down. Edgestitch up the tape for 12" (30 cm) for one tie, then stitch the tape around the neck edge. Edgestitch the next 12" and finish the raw edge.

4

Fold the bias tape down to the inside of the collar. Topstitch about 1/2" (12 mm) along the neckline to keep the bias inside the collar and form a neck band.

DESIGN
MARYN WYNNE

Clay Cat Ornaments

Materials

White or ivory polymer clay

Paper clips

Acrylic paint and fine paintbrushes

Heavy gold thread or thin braid

Sculpting or manicure tools

Antiquing medium

Satin spray polyurethane

Short length of gold bead trim and small gold stars (only for angel cat)

For Stocking Cat

1

Form a stocking shape about 2-1/2" (6 cm) long from clay. Press in designs with sculpting or manicuring tools. Add a 1-1/4" (4 cm) diameter circle of clay for the cat's head. Add ears and a muzzle, using the tools to shape and form the clay.

2

Add a clay bow at the neck and a stocking cap. Cut a paper clip in half to form a u-shaped wire hook. Push the cut edges of the clip into the top of the hat so that a 1/8" (3 mm) curved edge protrudes.

3

Bake the clay according to the manufacturer's instructions. Paint with acrylic paints as desired, then apply a coat of antiquing medium and a coat of protective polyurethane, allowing each coat to completely dry before adding the next. Tie a piece of gold thread onto the paper clip to form a hanger.

Angel Cat

1

Form a triangle of clay with a 3" (7.5 cm) base to form the dress. Add a 1" (2.5 cm) diameter circle of clay to form the head, then add ears and a muzzle and shape with tools.

2

Cut a paper clip in half to form a u-shaped wire hook. Push the cut edges of the clip into the top of the head so that a 1/8" curved edge protrudes.

3

Add 2" (5 cm) long wings and press details in with tools. Add a 1 x 1-1/2" (2.5 x 4 cm) piece of clay on each side to form sleeves and small circles for paws.

4

Bake and finish as directed in step 3 for the stocking cat. Glue the bead trim and a short length of gold thread around the bottom of the apron. Glue stars on top of the thread and under kitty's chin.

Pumpkin Cat

1

Form a 2-1/4" (6 cm) diameter circle of clay to form the pumpkin. Press in details with tools and shape. Add a small piece of clay to form the leaf.

2

Cut a paper clip in half to form a u-shaped wire hook. Push the cut edges of the clip into the top of the head so that a 1/8" (3 mm) curved edge protrudes.

3

Form a 1" (2.5 cm) diameter circle for the cat's head. Add ears, a muzzle, paws, and a tail, then shape with tools. Bake and finish as directed in step 3 for the stocking cat.

DESIGN
DOLLY LUTZ
MORRIS

Scrap Cat Baby Quilt

Light and dark fabric scraps, washed and pressed (1/8 yard yields approximately 3 cats and a 5x5" square of light fabric makes one cat background)

2-1/2 yards (2.3 m) border fabric, washed and pressed

1-1/2 yards (1.4 m) backing fabric, washed and pressed

30 x 50" (75 x 125 cm) rectangle of polyester batting

6-strand embroidery floss or #3 crochet cotton

Chenile needle

□ wrong side of fabric

□ right side of fabric

1

For each block, cut the following templates, adding seam allowances as reflected in the measurements.

1 from template A in background fabric (3-1/2 x 1-1/2", 9 x 4 cm)

1 from template D in background fabric (4-1/2 x 1-1/2", 11 x 4 cm)

1 from template F in background fabric (3-1/2 x 1-1/2", 9 x 4 cm)

2 from template B in cat fabric (1-1/2 x 1-1/2", 4 x 4 cm)

1 from template C in cat fabric (3-1/2 x 7-1/2", 9 x 19 cm)

1 from template E in cat fabric (5-1/2 x 1-1/2", 14 x 4 cm)

1 from template G in cat fabric (6-1/2 x 1-1/2", 16 x 4 cm)

2

Stitch rectangle D to rectangle E with right sides facing. Trim seam to 1/4" (6 mm) and press the seam toward the darker fabric. Stitch rectangle F to rectangle G. Trim and press. The assembled pieces should measure 1-1/2 x 8-1/2" (4 x 21 cm).

3

Complete the block as shown in the diagram, using 1/4" seam allowances on all sides. A finished cat block should measure 5-1/2 x 8-1/2" (14 x 21 cm). Make the desired number of left-facing cats, then reverse the body and tail sections as

shown to make right-facing cats. (You will need a total of 20 cat blocks to make this quilt. Additional cats can be added to make a larger quilt.) Sew all cat blocks together using a 1/4" seam allowance.

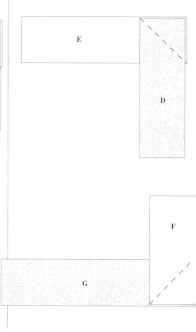

4

Cut 2 border strips measuring 4-1/2 x 40-1/2" (11 x 104 cm) and 2 strips measuring 4-1/2 x 28-1/2"(11 x 73 cm). Stitch the long strips to the sides and press the seams toward the darker side. Stitch the remaining strips to the top and bottom and press.

5

Place the backing fabric right side down on a flat surface. Place the batting on top of the fabric and center the quilt top over the batting with the cats facing up. Pin or baste the three layers together in several places to prevent shifting.

6

Thread the needle with embroidery floss or crochet cotton. Take asmall stitch through all three layers on the side you want the knots to show, leaving 2" (5 cm) tails for tying. Tie the tails in square knots and clip the tail ends to 1/2" (12 mm). Space the knots as directed by the batting manufacturer.

7

Cut 2" bias strips from the remaining border fabric and piece them at 45-degree angles to form 2 50" (125 cm) lengths and 2 30" (75 cm) lengths. Fold the strips in half lengthwise with wrong sides facing and press.

DESIGN
SUSAN DRISCOLL AND BOBBE NEEDHAM

8

Trim the excess batting and backing to within 1/4" of the quilt edge. Working on a flat surface, pin the binding to the long sides of the quilt with raw edges together. Fold the binding over the raw edges and pin the back side. Repeat with the top and bottom edges, adjusting at the corners. Blindstitch the binding on the back side to cover the seam line.

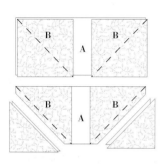

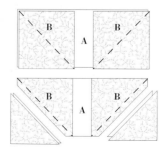

Why Do They Do That?

We purchased an elaborate scratching post for our cat's indoor use, so why does he keep scratching my brand new couch? Cats do need to scratch their nails to keep them sharp, but they also scratch to mark a territory, perhaps hoping to impress other cats with the height and depth of their claw marks. Unfortunately, most cat owners are not impressed with the height and depth of claw marks in their soft furnishings.

Why are cats so finicky? Cats develop a memory bank of the smells and tastes of acceptable foods during a relatively short time frame in early kittenhood. Usually, but not always, these acceptable foods are presented to the kittens by their mother. So, if a litter of kittens is born into your home and you've always fed their mother 9-Lives Fisherman's Feast, it's unlikely your kittens will refuse it. On the other hand, if you adopt a street cat who has eaten nothing but decaying meat scraps since its kitten days, you probably won't have much luck convincing it to eat boxed food from the grocery store.

Is my cat expressing her love for me when she rubs my legs and offers kitty kisses? Perhaps she is expressing love, but she's also marking you as her territory with scent glands on both side of her forehead.

Why do cats sleep so much? It's not your imagination: most cats sleep about 16 hours a day — about twice that of their human counterparts. As a species, cats have been dozing their days away for thousands of years, and many researchers believe this may be because cats are such efficient, successful hunters (unlike many other mammals) that they have lots of leftover time on their hands.

Why does my cat sink her claws into my legs when I pet her? The rhythmic kneading of your cat's paws when it's snuggled into your lap can be traced back to kittenhood, when your cat kneaded its mother's belly to stimulate milk flow. To your adult cat, your warmth may feel like their mother's body heat, while your petting may remind them of their mother's licking tongue. So don't catapult your cat from your lap the next time you're scratched. Take it as a compliment, then gently remove her claws.

> "CAT PEOPLE ARE DIFFERENT, TO THE EXTENT THAT THEY GENERALLY ARE NOT CONFORMISTS. HOW COULD THEY BE, WITH A CAT RUNNING THEIR LIVES?"
> — LOUIS CAMUTI

Fractured Feline Earrings

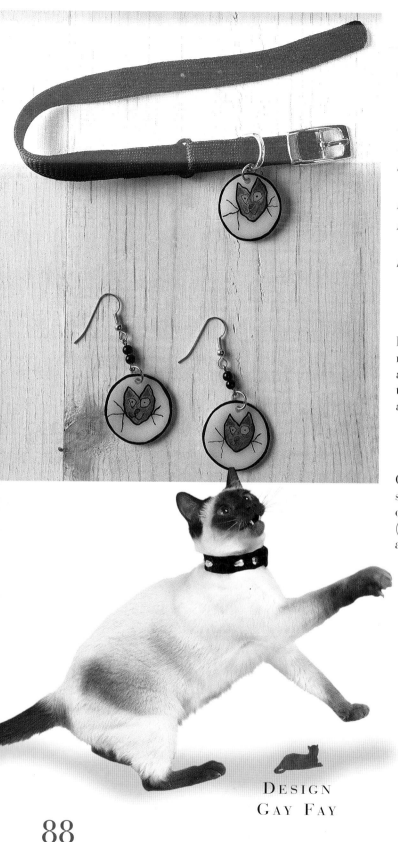

MATERIALS

Sheet of shrinkable plastic film (available in larger craft stores)

Large jump ring

Pair of ear clips or wires

Several colors of permanent markers

Hole punch

Needle-nose and round-nose pliers

Kitchen parchment paper

1

Place the plastic over the motif on page 123. Trace and fill in the colored areas, then trace the black lines and areas.

2

Cut out the circles. Make a small hole in the center top of each circle, about 1/8" (3 mm) from the edge with a hole punch.

3

Bake the circles in a pan lined with parchment paper according to the manufacturer's instructions. The plastic will soften and shrink as it bakes, eventually becoming the thickness of a nickel.

4

Allow the pieces to cool for 30 seconds, then lift them from the pan with a spatula and place them on a clean, flat surface to finish cooling.

5

Thread two 4-mm beads on a 5/8" (16 mm) eye pin and turn a loop to close. Repeat with a second pin. Hang the cat bead from the eye pin with a jump ring. Hang the assembled beads from the loop of an ear wire or post.

Note: For a matching cat collar, make an extra fractured cat bead, thread it on a large, soft jump ring, and hang it from the collar's D-ring.

DESIGN
GAY FAY

Charm Collars

MATERIALS

Strip of cotton fabric, 1-3/4" (5 cm) wide

40-50 seed beads

20-30 accent beads

Fish charm

Embroidery floss

Short length of sturdy elastic thread

Button

1

Measure the distance around your cat's neck and cut the fabric strip to this length plus 1" (2.5 cm) for ease. Press down a narrow hem allowance on the two short edges and one of the long edges.

2

Fold and press the unpressed long edge under about one-third of the width, then fold and press the remaining long edge over to create a narrow strip of fabric with no raw edges.

3

Unfold the fabric and embroider the middle section with several colors of thread and varying lengths of running stitches, picking up an occasional seed bead if desired. Add custom motifs, such as the fish skeletons on the collar at left, if desired. (See motif pattern on page 123.)

4

Form a loop with the elastic and tack it in place in the center of one end on the wrong side. Refold the fabric and slip stitch the seam. Sew the button in place.

DESIGN
MARY SAVAGE

Play Cats

MATERIALS

1/2 yard (.5 m) bright-colored fleece

3/4 yard (.75 m) cat-print cotton fabric

Scraps of neutral-colored fabric

Sewing pattern for button-down jacket or shirt with cuffs, and elastic pants

Embroidery floss, optional

Fusible web

Button covering kit

1

Cut out the shirt pattern from the fleece and assemble the front, back, and sleeve sections. Add cuffs in a cat-print pattern if desired. Finish the neck and bottom edges with a machine zigzag stitch or with a hand-stitched buttonhole edging with embroidery floss.

2

Select several sections of cat motifs and apply fusible web to each one according to the manufacturer's instructions. Cut away each cat, following the lines very carefully, then apply the cats to the shirt. Finish all edges with a narrow zigzag stitch.

3

Select small sections of the cat print for buttons. Use fusible web to back the print fabric with a neutral colored fabric. Assemble the buttons according to the kit instructions. Cut out and make a simple pair of elastic pants from the print fabric.

DESIGN
NANCY ASMUS

Playing Dress Up

What kind of people dress their pets in finery? "People who are truly connected with their animal," says Maryn Wynne, co-owner of Flytes of Fancy: Dog Togs & Feline Finery. "They're also people with a sense of humor." Maryn's company produces lighthearted, whimsical costumes and accessories for dressing up cats and dogs for birthday parties, parades, holidays, photo sessions, and just for the fun of it.

Maryn's mother and partner, Liz Fye, designs most of the costumes, while Maryn oversees production and develops new markets. "We strive to make the costumes comfortable and unrestricting, so we avoid doing full-body clothes," says Maryn. Liz does many of the initial feline fittings on her cat, Max. "He's a beautiful cat with a great personality. When I call him up to the table for a fitting, he sits there very patiently. He's so shy, though, that we've never been able to photograph him for a catalog."

"The best part about our business," agree Maryn and Liz, "is that it makes everybody laugh. We just love it when people look at our lines and break out laughing. And we love the stories and photos that people share with us. Pets truly enjoy the extra attention that costumes bring."

Kitty Dreams Blanket

MATERIALS

Lion Brand Jiffy, 3 skeins Denver (shaded blue, turquoise, violet, and pink, color #307) and 2 skeins Fisherman (color #99)

27" (67 cm) circular knitting needles size 10-1/2 or size to achieve correct gauge

Darning needle

GAUGE

15 stitches equals 4" (10 cm)

ABBREVIATIONS

st = stitch; tbl = through back of loop; wyif = with yarn in front (bring yarn to front between needles); wyib = with yarn in back

PATTERN NOTES

Always knit the first st of the row tbl. Always slip the last st of the row purlwise, with yarn in front; always slip as if to purl.

CHART NOTES

Each row of the graph equals two rows of mosaic knitting. Look at the graph on the right-side rows only. Each square of the graph equals one stitch. Use only one color of yarn at a time. Do not cut yarns; instead, pick them up when you need that color again. Check the block farthest to the right in each row and use that color for the next two rows of knitting. A shaded square equals Denver and an empty square equals Fisherman.

When a right-side row starts with a Denver square, knit all the Denver sts and slip all the Fisherman sts with yarn in the back. Turn. On the wrong side, knit all the Denver sts and slip all the Fisherman sts with yarn in front. When a right-side row starts with a Fisherman square, knit all the Fisherman sts and slip all the other sts with yarn in back. Turn. On the wrong side, knit all the Fisherman sts and slip all the other stitches with yarn in front.

1

Knit a swatch to double-check your gauge. Adjust your needle size if necessary.

15 sts should equal 4". Cast on 103 sts with Denver, turn. K 1st tbl, knit across to last st, slip last st wyif to complete the bottom row of the graph.

2

Attach Fisherman and begin working the graph on page 105 according to the notes above, reading right to left, the second row from the bottom. If you need help reading the graph, following are written instructions for the Fisherman rows: k 1st st tbl, k 1, sl 1 wyib, (k 1, sl3 wyib) 24 times, k1, sl 1 wyib, k1, sl 1 wyif. Turn. K 1st st tbl, then knit all the Fisherman sts and slip all the Denver sts wyif, to last st, sl last st wyif.

3

Continue working the graph in this manner until you have finished the graph. Bind off in Denver on the next row. Darn in ends.

Design
Suzann Thompson

Simple Collars

DESIGN
ALICE ENSLEY

MATERIALS

Length of trim compatible with your cat's personality or an upcoming holiday

Velcro strips in the same width as trim

Metallic or jewel studs, optional

Elastic, optional

1

Add 1-1/2" (4 cm) to your cat's neck measurement and cut the trim to this size. Fold down a narrow hem on each end and machine stitch.

2

Sew or adhere a 1-1/2" length of Velcro to the right side of the trim at one end. On the other end, sew or adhere the matched piece of Velcro to the wrong side of the trim. If desired, position and adhere metallic or jewel studs.

Note: For active, outdoor felines, cut the collar 2 - 3" (5 - 7 cm) longer. Stretch and stitch elastic to the back side so the collar will slip off if it gets caught on something.

MATERIALS FOR BLACK VEST

1-1/2 yards (1.4 m) black cotton fabric

1-1/2 yards red cotton fabric

7 colors of bright fabric scraps, approximately 1/8 yard (.1 m) each

Vest pattern with curved or pointed front edges

Freezer or tissue paper

Fusible webbing

Fabric paint, optional

1

Trace the front and back sections of your vest pattern onto freezer or tissue paper. Turn your front pattern piece over and trace it again so you end up with a right front and a left front.

2

Mark and cut the front and back pieces according to the illustrations. Number the pattern pieces as illustrated. Cut out the black fabric from these new patterns.

3

Cut a 1-1/2 x 22" (4 x 55 cm) strip from each of the scrap fabrics. Sew the strips together lengthwise. Press the seams open and then cut them into multicolored strips. (See illustration.)

4

Referring to the illustrations. pin multicolored strips between the sections and stitch in place. then assemble the pieces into front and back vest shapes.

5

Photocopy the cat motifs on page 103. enlarging if desired. Iron fusible web to the wrong side of your scrap fabrics according to the manufacturer's instructions. Pin the cat patterns onto the webbed fabric and cut out.

6

Position the cats and iron in place. Transfer the features onto the fabric. then finish the edges and features with a narrow zigzag stitch or with fabric paint. Use a tear-away backing fabric if you choose to finish the edges with zigzagging.

7

Place your original front and back patterns over your fabric and trim off any excess. Cut out the lining from the red fabric and then assemble the vest as directed in the pattern instructions.

MATERIALS FOR BROWN VEST

1-1/2 yards (1.4 m) brown cotton fabric

1-1/2 yards printed lining fabric

7 scraps of printed fabrics. approximately 1/8 yard (.1 m) each

Freezer or tissue paper

Vest pattern with curved or pointed front edges

Fusible webbing

Fabric paint, optional

1

Trace the front and back sections of your vest pattern onto freezer or tissue paper. Turn your front pattern piece over and trace it again so you end up with a right front and a left front.

2

Mark and cut the front and back pieces as indicated in the Bright Cat Vest instructions. Number the pattern pieces as illustrated. Cut out the brown fabric from these new patterns. adding 1/4" (6 mm) seam allowance to all cut edges of the pattern pieces.

3

Cut out five 2" (5 cm) fabric squares from each of the scrap fabrics. Fold the squares and press as shown in the illustrations, then stitch together in strips to match the seams. Pin the strips into the seams, referring to the assembly guideline shown in the Bright Cat instructions.

4

Enlarge the cat motifs on page 103 to the desired size and photocopy. Iron fusible web to the wrong side of your scrap fabrics according to the manufacturer's instructions. Pin the cat patterns onto the webbed fabric and cut out.

5

Position the cats and iron in place. Transfer the features onto the fabric, then finish the edges and features with a narrow zigzag stitch or with fabric paint. Use a tear-away backing fabric if you choose to finish the edges with zigzagging.

6

Place your original front and back patterns over your fabric and trim off any excess fabric. Cut out the lining fabric and assemble the vest as directed in the pattern instructions.

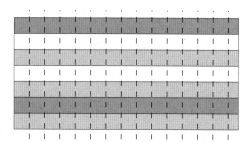

DESIGN
NANCY ASMUS

Fur Stocking

MATERIALS

1/2 yard (.5 m) green satin

1/2 yard red velvet

1/2 yard lining fabric

Scraps of solid ivory and black

Scraps of a cat print

1/4 yard (.2 m) fun fur

Thick upholstery cording

1/4 yard adhesive webbing

Fabric glue

Note: When cutting fur, always trace your image on the wrong side and outline the marks with sewing pins. Smooth the fur inside your lines on the right side and tape it down. Cut out and smooth fur back in place.

1

Cut out the stocking fabrics from the pattern on page 108. Cut a 1-1/2" (4 cm) wide strip of velvet on the bias long enough to go all the way around the stocking.

2

Cut the scrap fabrics into squares or rectangles large enough to accommodate the motifs. Attach the adhesive bonding as directed by the manufacturer and cut out the motifs. Attach the cat's head, facial features, and hat to the stocking front, then add the fur.

3

Place the bias strip on a flat surface with its right side facing down. Place the cording in the center of the strip and fold in half lengthwise. Secure with basting stitches.

4

Pin the cording to the stocking front, positioning the pins horizontally, then pin the stocking back to the front with right sides facing. Trim and clip the seams; turn right sides out.

5

Pin and stitch the lining fabrics with right sides facing. Trim the seams and turn right sides out. Insert the lining into the stocking and smooth in place. Pin the lining to the stocking at the top edge.

6

Cut a 1 x 5" (2.5 x 13 cm) strip of velvet on the bias. Fold in half lengthwise and stitch with a 1/4" (6 mm) seam allowance. Turn right sides out and thread a length of cording through the tube. Fold the tube in half to form a hanging loop and stitch the raw edges to the back side of the stocking.

7

Cut a fur strip 4" (10 cm) high and long enough to fit around the cuff plus 1". Fold the trim over the raw edges at the top and glue in place, positioning the ends on the hanging side and fluffing the fur to disguise the seam.

My-Favorite-Things Kitty Stocking

MATERIALS

1/2 yard (.5 m) main fabric

1/2 yard lining fabric

Scraps of 8 print fabrics, one in a color and print suitable for a tree and one in a holiday print

1/4 yard (.2 m) fusible adhesive webbing

Gold embroidery floss

14" (35 cm) length of miniature tree trim lights

Fabric marker

Metallic green thread

Small ball of yarn in a holiday color

Tapestry needle

Craft glue

1

Cut out the stocking pieces from the patterns on page 109. Cut out squares or rectangles slightly larger than the motifs and attach adhesive webbing to the backs as directed in the manufacturer's instructions. Cut out the motifs from the adhesive-backed fabrics.

2

Position and adhere the heel and toe trims and the tree onto the stocking front. Position and adhere the star, mouse, butterfly, bird, dragonfly, fish, and lizard onto the tree.

3

Stitch or glue the miniature tree lights down the tree so they connect the animals. Embroider a French knot at each star point. Add features to the animals with a fabric marker. To make the mouse's curly tail, coat the bottom 2" (5 cm) of a 15" (37 cm) length of embroidery floss in craft glue and wrap it in even intervals around a wooden cooking skewer or similar object. Slide the yarn off, trim the curled portion to an appropriate tail length, and stitch in place.

4

Secure a small yarn ball in place with several stitches on the back side, leaving a 10" (25 cm) tail of unwound yarn. Loop the tail up toward the tree, securing on the underside with small stitches as needed. Thread the yarn on a tapestry needle, run the yarn to the back side, and tie off.

5

Create a striped band for the stocking's cuff by sewing 15 1-1/2 × 1" (4 × 2.5 cm) strips of fabric together. Press all seams open. Stitch the cuff to the stocking front and press.

6

Stitch the lining pieces together with wrong sides facing. Place a stocking front and back on either side of the lining with right sides facing out.

7

Begin pinning the binding at the top right side, securing all four stocking layers together, and continue pinning until you reach the bottom of the cuff on the adjacent side. Stop pinning and leave a 6" (15 cm) tail of binding.

8

Pin and stitch the binding around the top of the stocking, covering the raw edge of the binding on the right side. Continue pinning the binding up the left side of the stocking, covering the raw edge at the top left. Machine stitch the open side edges of the binding tail together. Form a 2" (5 cm) loop with the binding and stitch down on the back side.

DESIGN
LEAH NALL

Cat Food Jewelry

MATERIALS

Package of caramel-colored polymer clay

Package of block ochre-colored polymer clay

Pinch of golden yellow-colored polymer clay

Craft knife

Sheet of coarse sandpaper, torn into strips

Smooth rubber gloves, optional

12" (30 cm) length of wire

French ear wires designed to accommodate a drop

12 accent beads

2 head pins

12 eye pins

4 jump rings

Round nose pliers

1

Work the clay in your hands until it becomes pliable. (An incandescent light very close to your work area can help soften the clay.)

2

Form a 1/4" (6 mm) diameter ball of caramel clay and flatten it to 1/2" (12 mm) in diameter. Cut out a rough "+" shape with a craft knife. Remove the excess clay. Use strips of coarse sandpaper to shape and add texture to each arm of the cat food stars. Repeat five times.

3

Add a pinch of golden yellow clay to the ochre clay and form triangular shapes between your thumbs and index fingers, wearing rubber gloves to prevent fingerprints if desired.

4

Pierce each cat food bead with a sewing needle or thin piece of wire. The triangular beads should be pierced

through the center of the clay, while the "t" shaped beads can be pierced through the center or at the tip of one protrusion. String the beads onto a thin piece of wire and bake them in the oven according the manufacturer's instructions.

5

Thread the beads onto eye pins in small groupings, using the photo as a guide or creating your own arrangement. Thread the bottom beads onto head pins or jump rings, depending on where you positioned the bead holes. Attach the groupings together, bending the ends into loops and threading them through the adjacent loop, then attach the groupings to the top jump ring and the jump ring to the jewelry finding.

DESIGN
VAN THOMPSON

101

Cat Fur Hat

Cat hair
Crochet or knitting hat
 pattern
Small hook or needles

1

Collect a grocery-store size plastic bag of cat fur. Biweekly brushings are the easiest way to gather hair.

2

Take the fur to a yarn spin-ner or enroll in a spinning workshop. (It's a simple process to learn — really) Cat fur spins with the same technique as sheep wool, but the hands should be kept closer together since the hairs are shorter and finer than wool.

3

Search out a beret-style cro-chet or knitting hat pattern with little or no openwork. Work a swatch with a small hook or needles to check the gauge, then crochet or knit as usual.

DESIGN
GENNA MILES

Photocopy at 200%.

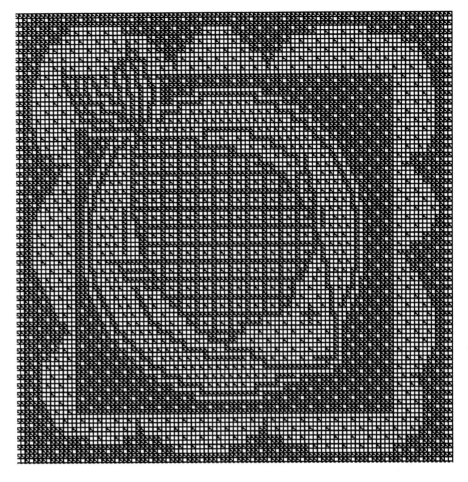

105

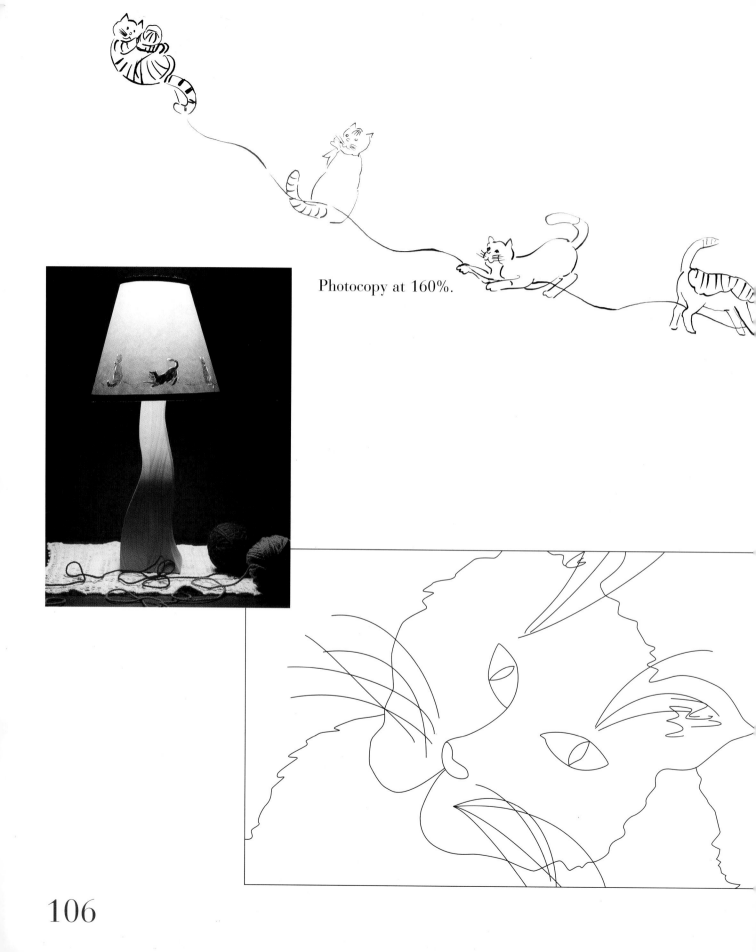

Photocopy at 160%.

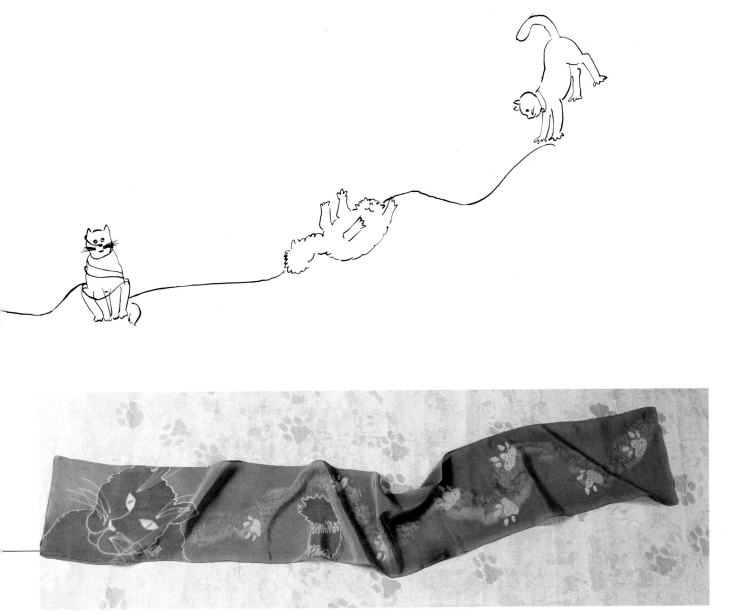

Photocopy at 200%.

Photocopy at 250%.

Sailor Collar
(cut 2)

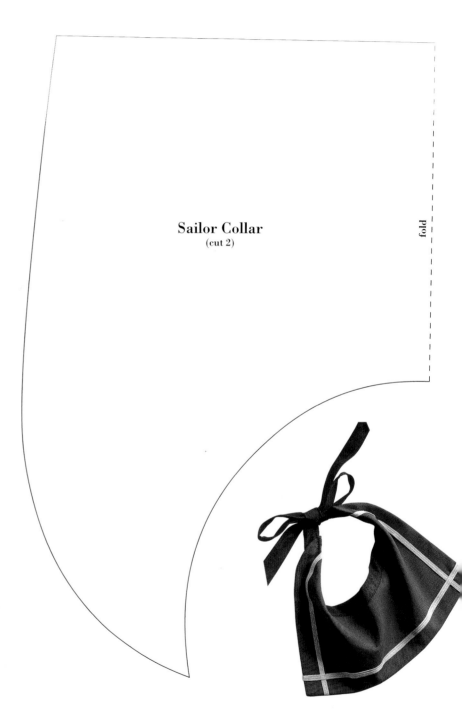

111

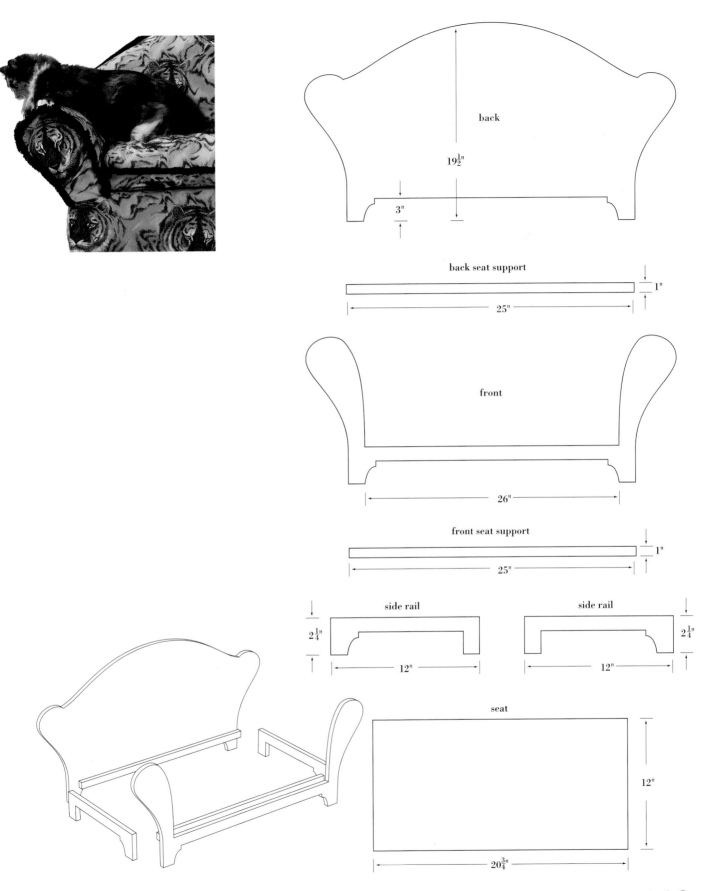

back

$19\frac{1}{2}$"

3"

back seat support

1"

25"

front

26"

front seat support

1"

25"

side rail

side rail

$2\frac{1}{4}$"

$2\frac{1}{4}$"

12"

12"

seat

12"

$20\frac{3}{4}$"

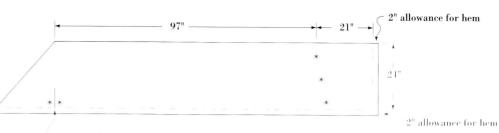

97"   21"   2" allowance for hem

21"

2" allowance for hem

approx. placement for rear view mirrors

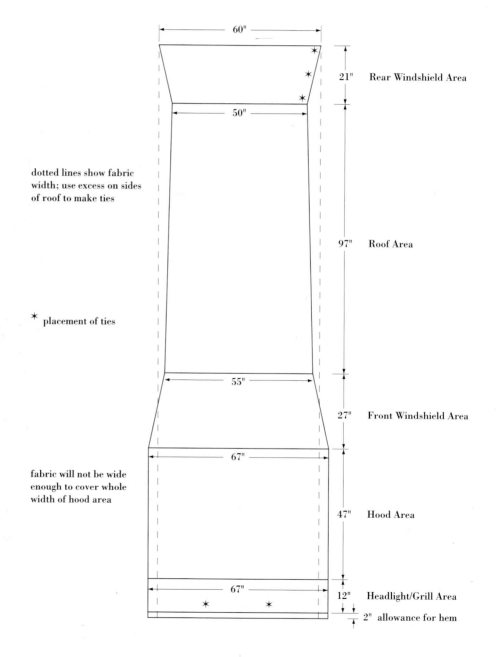

60"

21"   Rear Windshield Area

50"

dotted lines show fabric
width; use excess on sides
of roof to make ties

97"   Roof Area

✳ placement of ties

55"

27"   Front Windshield Area

67"

fabric will not be wide
enough to cover whole
width of hood area

47"   Hood Area

67"

12"   Headlight/Grill Area

2" allowance for hem

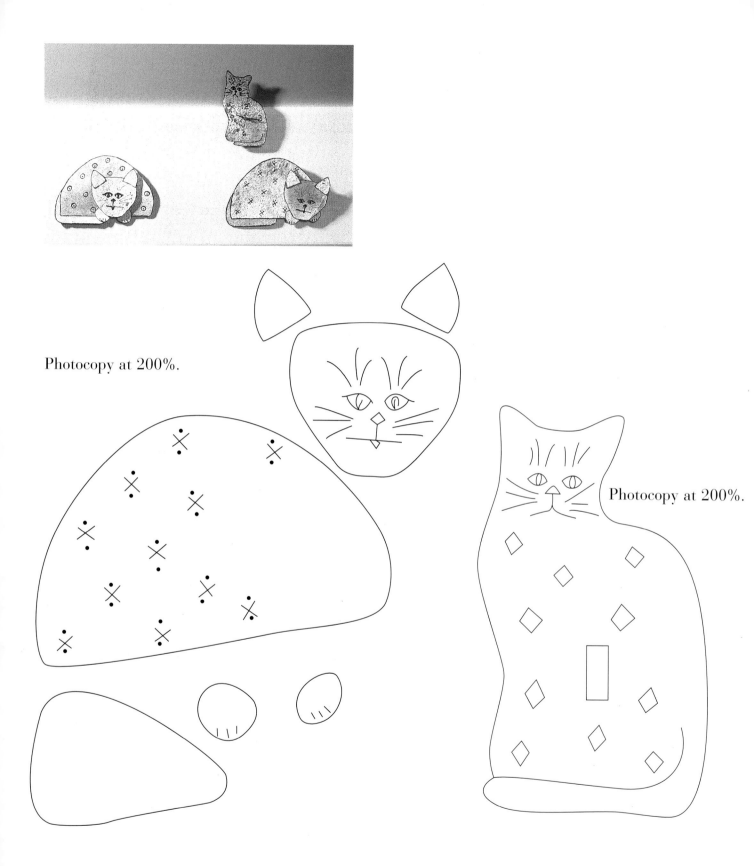

Photocopy at 200%.

Photocopy at 200%.

116

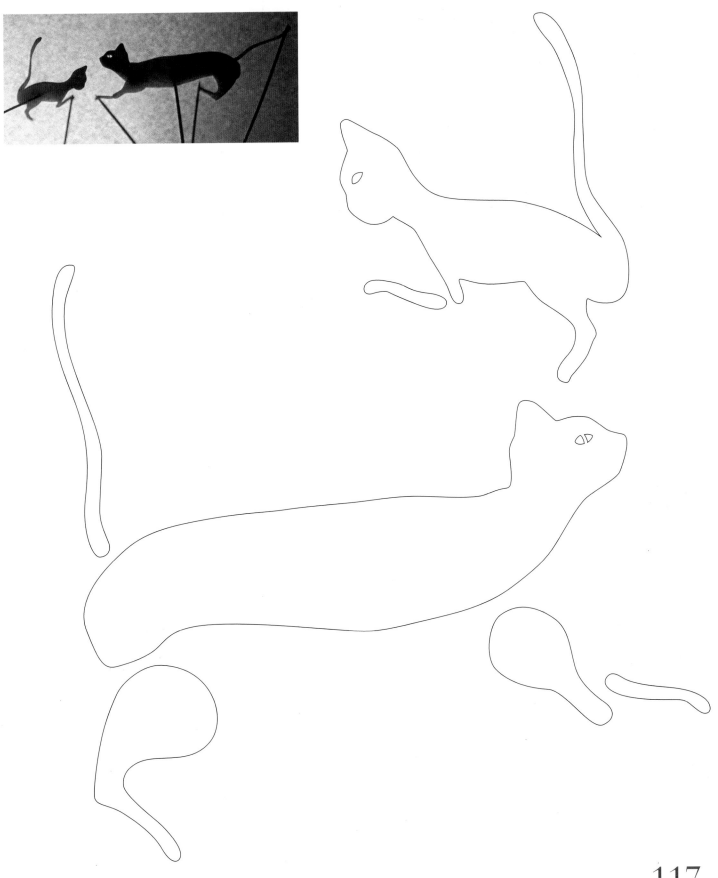

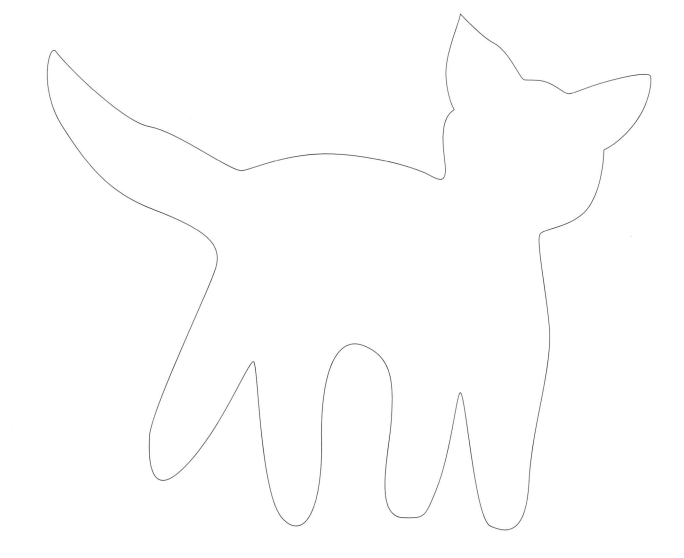

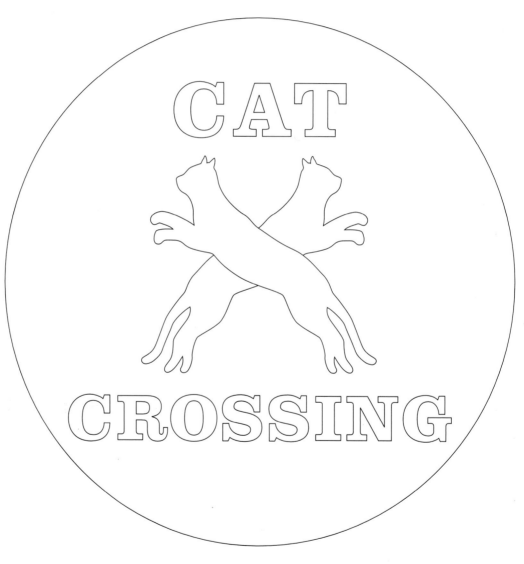

Photocopy at 200%.

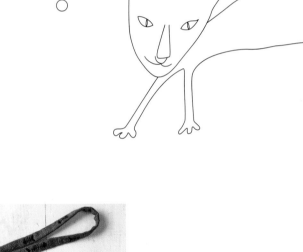

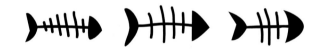

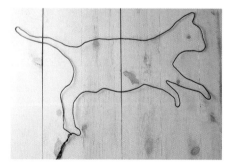

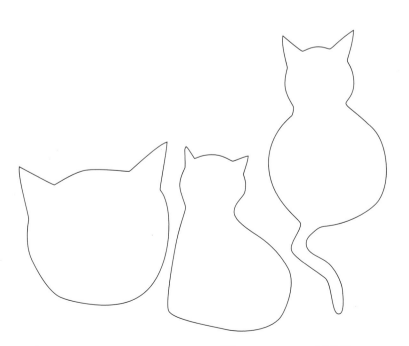

Photocopy at 125%.

Index